# Liberalism:
# A Socio-Economic Exposition

*By Ludwig von Mises*

*Foreword to the Second Edition by*
*Louis M. Spadaro*

*Translated by Ralph Raico*
*Edited by Arthur Goddard*

SHEED ANDREWS AND McMEEL, INC.
Subsidiary of Universal Press Syndicate
Kansas City

This edition is published in cooperation with the programs of the Institute for Humane Studies, Inc., Menlo Park, California; and Liberty Fund, Inc., Indianapolis, Indiana.

*Liberalism: A Socio-Economic Exposition*
Copyright © 1962 by William Volker Fund as *The Free and Prosperous Commonwealth: An Exposition of the Ideas of Classical Liberalism.*
Copyright assigned to the Institute for Humane Studies, Inc., 1976.
Foreword to Second Edition Copyright © 1978 by the Institute for Humane Studies, Inc.

Jacket and cover designs by Design Center, Inc., Indianapolis. Copyright © 1978 by the Institute for Humane Studies.

**Library of Congress Cataloging in Publication Data**
Von Mises, Ludwig, 1881-1973.
    Liberalism.

    (Studies in economic theory)
    Translation of Liberalismus.
    Published in 1962 under title: The free and prosperous commonwealth.
    Includes index.
    1. Liberalism. 2. Economics. I. Goddard, Arthur. II. Title. III. Series.
JC585.V613  1978   320.5'12      78-8457
ISBN 0-8362-5107-5
ISBN 0-8362-5106-7 pbk.

# Foreword

The importance of this little book is far greater, I believe, than one would expect from its modest size and unpretentious language. It is, very simply, a book about the free society; about what would now-a-days be termed the "policy implications" for such a society in the conduct of both its internal and external affairs; and very especially about some of the obstacles and problems, whether real or imagined, lying in the way of establishing and maintaining that form of social organization.

Now, while there is nothing extraordinary in all this, the surprising fact is that virtually none of those who have advocated some alternative form of social economic organization offered a similar discussion of their respective proposals. Even now, the growing band of writers who regale us with detailed criticisms of capitalism and with forecasts of its impending demise are strangely reticent in treating any "contradictions" or other difficulties that might occur in the operation of the system they prefer or predict.

The significance of this omission, however, has too easily been brushed aside only because the responsibility for it is usually somewhat misplaced. To accuse Marx—to take the most frequent example—of failure to describe the operating details and the implications of a socialist society in *Das Kapital* is indefensible; for that work is exactly what it was intended to be: a highly critical examination of the workings of capitalism as Marx conceived the latter to be. It would be just as vacuous to accuse Mises of neglecting to include, in his *Socialism,* a discussion of the principles of an enterprise system. But the essential point is that Mises *did* address himself to just such a task in a separate book—this one—whereas Marx never did. This, then, is the book which Marx failed to write and which his followers and other critics of liberalism also neglected to do.

The real importance of this book, however, is not to be found in this narrower and more polemical sense, but in a much more fundamental and constructive one. Despite its brevity, this essay manages to speak to a fairly large number of the questions, doubts, and confusions most people face in the course of making up their minds on controversial—often emotional—social and economic issues. Its particular merit is that on all of the questions taken up, Mises provides insights and alternative views that are sure to be useful.

Since the reader will surely want to proceed at once to examine and consider some of these, I shall not intrude with comments of my own, except for one or two irrepressible reflections with which this foreword will close. Instead, we shall next take up a sampling of those questions and opinions commonly on the minds of people considering controversial issues on which Mises has things to say here that are worth taking into account. For convenience, these are listed more or less in the order in which reference to them occurs in the text.

1. The free market system has been in full operation, and over a long time, but has proved to be unworkable.
2. Liberalism suffers from a fixation on the desirability of increasing production and material well-being and persistently overlooks man's spiritual needs.
3. Since people don't always act perfectly rationally, might we not do better, on some issues, to put less reliance on strictly logical arguments and to trust more to our intuitions, impulses, and so-called "gut" feelings?
4. There can be no denying that capitalism is essentially a system that is structured to favor the rich and propertied people at the expense of other classes.
5. Why defend a social system that does not enable each and every individual to realize what he dreams of, or to achieve everything he works for?
6. Is the private ownership of the means of production an obso-

lete piece of "excess baggage" carried over from earlier periods by people who find it difficult to accept and accommodate to changed conditions?

7. By its very nature, doesn't a competitive market economy at best tend to work against international peace, and at worst, actually to promote wars?

8. What possible defense can there be for a socio-economic system that produces such great inequalities in income and consumption?

9. Pragmatism aside, can there be a *morally* defensible justification for private property rights?

10. In opposing government interventions, is Liberalism not implicitly bound to advocate some form of anarchy in the end?

11. It is not self-evident that a stable, democratic society is any more possible under a system of decentralized planning and decision-making than under a centrally planned economy.

12. What reason is there to expect that a capitalist society will necessarily be any more tolerant of dissension than a socialist one?

13. Capitalism creates and preserves a preferential position for a "leisure class" of resource owners who do not work or contribute in any significant way to the society.

14. The reason the institution of private property has survived for so long is that it has been protected by the state; indeed, as Marx argued, the preservation of private property is the one and only function of the state.

15. The argument that socialism cannot work by itself because it lacks the means of making the required economic calculations is interesting, but are there specific, concrete illustrations of this?

16. Also interesting is the suggestion that government interventions in the operation of private enterprise necessarily lead to distortions and are therefore self-defeating, but can it be shown by specific example that this is necessarily the case?

17. Apart from arguing that alternative proposed systems can be shown to be inferior, are there any direct and positive reasons for advocating a free-enterprise system?

18. Since in order to be workable, an enterprise system requires a large number of relatively small firms in very active competition with each other, has it not been rendered largely obsolete by the development of giant corporations, monopolies, and the like?
19. Inasmuch as the managements of large corporations tend to develop into bureaucracies, too, isn't the issue of private versus public control largely a distinction without a difference?
20. Is the co-ordination between domestic and foreign policies any more feasible or consistent under Liberalism than under some other system?
21. Isn't the existence and protection of rights of private ownership a hindrance rather than a help in achieving and maintaining international peace and understanding?
22. It seems obvious that nationalism, colonialism, and imperialism could have evolved only under capitalism.
23. The self-interest of private enterprises is the main impediment in the way of developing a freer movement of goods and people among the world's regions.
24. Since it represents and fosters the special interests of one class—the resource-owners or capitalists—Liberalism made a serious tactical blunder in not constituting itself a political party and in not pursuing its aims through compromises and in accordance with political expediency.

Anyone who has been in a position to observe at close range how certain presuppositions, half-truths, and seemingly self-evident "values" often prevent people from giving full and fair considerations to unfamiliar or unfashionable views in economics will recognize many of the points mentioned in this list. What Mises has to say on each of these should help the general reader (and the beginning student) toward a more comprehensive perspective on social issues and also to deal with his own doubts and suspicions. The suppression of the book in East Germany, to which Mises refers in his preface becomes understandable in this light and is another—and unintended—indication of its importance.

Finally, there are two points on which I should like to make some brief comment. The first is one which recurs a number of times in the book but in such very different contexts and so far apart that its generality and importance may not be noticed.

This is the idea—so essential to the logic of true Liberalism—that it is often wise and productive to make what Mises in one place calls "provisional sacrifices." To claim an immediate benefit, however attractive it may seem, is an act of folly, if, by so doing, one shuts off a disproportionately greater later benefit; that is, one so much greater that it more than makes up both for forgoing the present gain *and* for the trouble of waiting.

Of course, few reasonable people making this sort of "calculation" would be likely to choose the present benefit under the conditions stipulated. But—and this is the heart of the difficulty—people sometimes do not calculate prudently, nor are they encouraged to do so. The same type of omission occurs under very different circumstances and is far from being true only of the "ordinary" citizen or consumer. It may apply to businessmen in their pursuit of short-run profits or competitive advantage; to the legislator who favors an immediate increase in minimum-wage rates, in social security benefits, in tariffs, or other taxes; to economists who counsel increasing the money supply or a redistribution of incomes; and to an endless list of others. Indeed, it would be an excellent exercise for the reader to search for further examples both in the major sections of the present book and especially in thinking about contemporary issues and controversies.

Finally, a word of explanation is called for concerning the title of the book. The original work, published in 1927, was entitled *Liberalismus* and so complemented, as indicated earlier, Mises' book on socialism. That it was deemed desirable or necessary, when the English translation was prepared in the early sixties, to re-title it *The Free and Prosperous Commonwealth* illustrates pointedly what I believe to be a real tragedy in intellectual history: the transfer of the term Liberalism.

The underlying issue is not merely terminological; nor can it be brushed aside as just another instance of the more general degradation of language—an entropy of words, so to say—in which earlier distinctions of meaning and tonality have tended to be lost. There is more here than a devaluation of terms, important as that may be; involved are substantive matters of the greatest practical as well as intellectual significance.

To begin with, the word "liberal" has clear and pertinent etymological roots grounded in the ideal of individual liberty. It also has a valuable historical foundation in tradition and experience, as well as the patrimony of a rich and extensive literature in social philosophy, political thought, belles-lettres, and elsewhere. For these and many other reasons, it is inconceivable that the point of view which this book illustrates should not have exclusive and unassailable claim on the liberal label.

Yet, for all of this, the term Liberalism proved unable to go beyond the nineteenth century or the Atlantic without changing its meaning—and not just slightly, but virtually to that of its contrary! The resulting confusions and imprecision are such that one finds it hard to conceive of a deliberate plan that could have succeeded more in obfuscating its content and meaning.

The sadness of all this is compounded by at least two more considerations. One is the astonishing agreeableness with which the titular heirs of liberalism not only let the title slip away, but actually repelled it by their willingness to use it as a term of opprobrium for crypto-Socialists, for whom a more relevant label already existed. In comparison to this spectacle, the ancient fable of the Camel and the Tent looks like a mild case of re-zoning.

The other reason for regret is that the loss of the term "liberal" made it necessary to have recourse to any number of contrived surrogate terms or tortured circumlocutions (e.g. "libertarian," "nineteenth century liberalism," or "classical" liberalism. Is there, incidentally, a *"neo*-classical" liberalism to which anyone claims membership?).

Is the liberal label by now irreversibly lost to us? In an appendix to the original German edition (and included in the translation), Mises discusses the changing meaning of the term and alludes to the possibility of recapturing it. But by 1962, in his preface to the English translation, he appears to have abandoned any hope of doing so.

I must respectfully disagree. Because, by any reasonable standard, Liberalism belongs to us, I believe we are bound to try to take it back—as a matter of principle, if for no other reason. And there *are* other reasons. For one thing, inasmuch as Liberalism, as Mises points out, includes more than economic freedom, it is really needed as the most suitable and inclusive term. For another, the need to communicate clearly and unambiguously with the general public—whose support is ultimately essential—we need a single, straightforward term and not some verbal contrivance that must sound "mealy-mouthed" to the man in the street. Furthermore, the present time and circumstances are relatively propitious—a growing general disenchantment with government interventions and the reviving awareness of individual freedom of choice can identify more readily with a respected and comprehensive name.

How can we proceed to reclaim our own name? Most probably by simply reversing the process by which we have been losing it; first by ceasing ourselves using it in its incorrect meaning; then by insistently re-inforcing its correct use (the term has not completely passed over in some parts of the world); and finally by refusing as often as is necessary to go along with its continued occupancy by those with less than no legitimate claim to it—they should be urged to seek a label that fits their views as well as Liberalism does ours.

Some will fret unduly about the inevitable confusion of doctrines—I suspect this concern was partly responsible for our earlier unseemly haste in vacating the tent—but this is a price we should be ready to pay this time. For one thing, some confusion still exists as matters stand now, so that a bit more, temporarily, is not intolerable. Also, confusion cuts both ways, so others will share the cost— and this time, perhaps, the discomfort will cause the *camel* to withdraw.

Thus it is that the present reprint reverts to the original title of the book. It is to be hoped that others will concur in using the term without apology or qualification—it needs none—so that Liberalism may ultimately resume its traditional and correct meaning.

Louis M. Spadaro
Fordham University, August, 1977

# Preface to
# the English-Language Edition

The social order created by the philosophy of the Enlightenment assigned supremacy to the common man. In his capacity as
a consumer, the "regular fellow" was called upon to determine
ultimately what should be produced, in what quantity and of
what quality, by whom, how, and where; in his capacity as a
voter, he was sovereign in directing his nation's policies. In the
precapitalistic society those had been paramount who had the
strength to beat their weaker fellows into submission. The much
decried "mechanism" of the free market leaves only one way open
to the acquisition of wealth, viz., to succeed in serving the consumers in the best possible and cheapest way. To this "democracy"
of the market corresponds, in the sphere of the conduct of affairs
of state, the system of representative government. The greatness
of the period between the Napoleonic Wars and the first World
War consisted precisely in the fact that the social ideal after the
realization of which the most eminent men were striving was
free trade in a peaceful world of free nations. It was an age of
unprecedented improvement in the standard of living for a
rapidly increasing population. It was the age of liberalism.

Today the tenets of this nineteenth-century philosophy of liberalism are almost forgotten. In continental Europe it is remem-
bered only by a few. In England the term "liberal" is mostly used
to signify a program that only in details differs from the totali-
tarianism of the socialists.* In the United States "liberal" means
today a set of ideas and political postulates that in every regard
are the opposite of all that liberalism meant to the preceding

* Yet one should mention the fact that a few eminent Englishmen continue
to espouse the cause of genuine liberalism.

generations. The American self-styled liberal aims at government omnipotence, is a resolute foe of free enterprise, and advocates all-round planning by the authorities, i.e., socialism. These "liberals" are anxious to emphasize that they disapprove of the Russian dictator's policies not on account of their socialistic or communistic character but merely on account of their imperialistic tendencies. Every measure aiming at confiscating some of the assets of those who own more than the average or at restricting the rights of the owners of property is considered as liberal and progressive. Practically unlimited discretionary power is vested in government agencies the decisions of which are exempt from judicial review. The few upright citizens who dare to criticize this trend toward administrative despotism are branded as extremists, reactionaries, economic royalists, and Fascists. It is suggested that a free country ought not to tolerate political activities on the part of such "public enemies."

Surprisingly enough, these ideas are in this country viewed as specifically American, as the continuation of the principles and the philosophy of the Pilgrim Fathers, the signers of the Declaration of Independence, and the authors of the Constitution and the Federalist papers. Only few people realize that these allegedly progressive policies originated in Europe and that their most brilliant nineteenth-century exponent was Bismarck, whose policies no American would qualify as progressive and liberal. Bismarck's *Sozialpolitik* was inaugurated in 1881, more than fifty years before its replica, F. D. Roosevelt's New Deal. Following in the wake of the German Reich, the then most successful power, all European industrial nations more or less adopted the system that pretended to benefit the masses at the expense of a minority of "rugged individualists." The generation that reached voting age after the end of the first World War took statism for granted and had only contempt for the "bourgeois prejudice," liberty.

When, thirty-five years ago, I tried to give a summary of the ideas and principles of that social philosophy that was once known under the name of liberalism, I did not indulge in the vain hope that my account would prevent the impending catastrophes to which the policies adopted by the European nations were manifestly leading. All I wanted to achieve was to offer to the small minority of thoughtful people an opportunity to learn something about the aims of classical liberalism and its achievements and thus to pave the way for a resurrection of the spirit of freedom *after* the coming debacle.

On October 28, 1951, Professor T. P. Hamilius of Luxembourg ordered a copy of *Liberalismus* from the publishing firm of Gustav Fischer in Jena (Russian Zone of Germany). The publishing firm answered, on November 14, 1951, that no copies of the book were available and added: "Die Vorräte dieser Schrift mussten auf Anordnung behördlicher Stellen restlos makuliert werden." (By order of the authorities all the copies of this book had to be destroyed.) The letter did not say whether the "authorities" referred to were those of Nazi Germany or those of the "democratic" republic of East Germany.

In the years that elapsed since the publication of *Liberalismus* I have written much more about the problems involved. I have dealt with many issues with which I could not deal in a book the size of which had to be limited in order not to deter the general reader. On the other hand, I referred in it to some matters that have little importance for the present. There are, moreover, in this book various problems of policy treated in a way which can be understood and correctly appreciated only if one takes into account the political and economic situation at the time in which it was written.

I have not changed anything in the original text of the book and did not influence in any way the translation made by Dr. Ralph Raico and the editing done by Mr. Arthur Goddard. I am very grateful to these two scholars for the pains they took in making the book available to the English-reading public.

Ludwig von Mises
New York, April, 1962

# Contents

xvii

# Contents

# Introduction

## 1. *Liberalism*

The philosophers, sociologists, and economists of the eighteenth and the early part of the nineteenth century formulated a political program that served as a guide to social policy first in England and the United States, then on the European continent, and finally in the other parts of the inhabited world as well. Nowhere was this program ever completely carried out. Even in England, which has been called the homeland of liberalism and the model liberal country, the proponents of liberal policies never succeeded in winning all their demands. In the rest of the world only parts of the liberal program were adopted, while others, no less important, were either rejected from the very first or discarded after a short time. Only with some exaggeration can one say that the world once lived through a liberal era. Liberalism was never permitted to come to full fruition.

Nevertheless, brief and all too limited as the supremacy of liberal ideas was, it sufficed to change the face of the earth. A magnificent economic development took place. The release of man's productive powers multiplied the means of subsistence many times over. On the eve of the World War (which was itself the result of a long and bitter struggle against the liberal spirit and which ushered in a period of still more bitter attacks on liberal principles), the world was incomparably more densely populated than it had ever been, and each inhabitant could live incomparably better than had been possible in earlier centuries.

1

The prosperity that liberalism had created reduced considerably infant mortality, which had been the pitiless scourge of earlier ages, and, as a result of the improvement in living conditions, lengthened the average span of life.

Nor did this prosperity flow only to a select class of privileged persons. On the eve of the World War the worker in the industrial nations of Europe, in the United States, and in the overseas dominions of England lived better and more graciously than the nobleman of not too long before. Not only could he eat and drink according to his desire; he could give his children a better education; he could, if he wished, take part in the intellectual and cultural life of his nation; and, if he possessed enough talent and energy, he could, without difficulty, raise his social position. It was precisely in the countries that had gone the farthest in adopting the liberal program that the top of the social pyramid was composed, in the main, not of those who had, from their very birth, enjoyed a privileged position by virtue of the wealth or high rank of their parents, but of those who, under favorable conditions, had worked their way up from straitened circumstances by their own power. The barriers that had in earlier ages separated lords and serfs had fallen. Now there were only citizens with equal rights. No one was handicapped or persecuted on account of his nationality, his opinions, or his faith. Domestic political and religious persecutions had ceased, and international wars began to become less frequent. Optimists were already hailing the dawn of the age of eternal peace.

But events have turned out otherwise. In the nineteenth century strong and violent opponents of liberalism sprang up who succeeded in wiping out a great part of what had been gained by the liberals. The world today wants to hear no more of liberalism. Outside England the term "liberalism" is frankly proscribed. In England, there are, to be sure, still "liberals," but most of them are so in name only. In fact, they are rather moderate socialists. Everywhere today political power is in the hands of the antiliberal parties. The program of antiliberalism unleashed the forces that gave rise to the great World War and, by virtue of import and export quotas, tariffs, migration barriers, and similar measures, has brought the nations of the world to the point of mutual isolation. Within each nation it has led to socialist experiments whose result has been a reduction in the productivity of labor and a concomitant increase in want and misery. Whoever does not deliberately close his eyes to the facts must recognize everywhere the signs of an approaching catastrophe in world economy. Antiliberalism is heading toward a general collapse of civilization.

If one wants to know what liberalism is and what it aims at, one cannot simply turn to history for the information and inquire what the liberal politicians stood for and what they accomplished. For liberalism nowhere succeeded in carrying out its program as it had intended.

Nor can the programs and actions of those parties that today call themselves liberal provide us with any enlightenment concerning the nature of true liberalism. It has already been mentioned that even in England what is understood as liberalism today bears a much greater resemblance to Toryism and socialism than to the old program of the freetraders. If there are liberals who find it compatible with their liberalism to endorse the nationalization of railroads, of mines, and of other enterprises, and even to support protective tariffs, one can easily see that nowadays nothing is left of liberalism but the name.

Nor does it any longer suffice today to form one's idea of liberalism from a study of the writings of its great founders. Liberalism is not a completed doctrine or a fixed dogma. On the contrary: it is the application of the teachings of science to the social life of man. And just as economics, sociology, and philosophy have not stood still since the days of David Hume, Adam Smith, David Ricardo, Jeremy Bentham, and Wilhelm Humboldt, so the doctrine of liberalism is different today from what it was in their day, even though its fundamental principles have remained unchanged. For many years now no one has undertaken to present a concise statement of the essential meaning of that doctrine. This may serve to justify our present attempt at providing just such a work.

## 2. *Material Welfare*

Liberalism is a doctrine directed entirely towards the conduct of men in this world. In the last analysis, it has nothing else in view than the advancement of their outward, material welfare and does not concern itself directly with their inner, spiritual and metaphysical needs. It does not promise men happiness and contentment, but only the most abundant possible satisfaction of all those desires that can be satisfied by the things of the outer world.

Liberalism has often been reproached for this purely external and materialistic attitude toward what is earthly and transitory. The life of man, it is said, does not consist in eating and drinking. There are higher and more important needs than food and drink, shelter and clothing. Even the greatest earthly riches cannot give man happiness; they leave his inner self, his soul, unsatisfied and empty. The most serious error of liberalism has been that it has had nothing to offer man's deeper and nobler aspirations.

But the critics who speak in this vein show only that they have a very imperfect and materialistic conception of these higher and nobler needs. Social policy, with the means that are at its disposal, can make men rich or poor, but it can never succeed in making them happy or in satisfying their inmost yearnings. Here all external expedients fail. All that social policy can do is to remove the outer causes of pain and suffering; it can further a system that feeds the hungry, clothes the naked, and houses the homeless. Happiness and contentment do not depend on food, clothing, and shelter, but, above all, on what a man cherishes within himself. It is not from a disdain of spiritual goods that liberalism concerns itself exclusively with man's material well-being, but from a conviction that what is highest and deepest in man cannot be touched by any outward regulation. It seeks to produce only outer well-being because it knows that inner, spiritual riches cannot come to man from without, but only from within his own heart. It does not aim at creating anything but the outward preconditions for the development of the inner life. And there can be no doubt that the relatively prosperous individual of the twentieth century can more readily satisfy his spiritual needs than, say, the individual of the tenth century, who was given no respite from anxiety over the problem of eking out barely enough for survival or from the dangers that threatened him from his enemies.

To be sure, to those who, like the followers of many Asiatic and medieval Christian sects, accept the doctrine of complete asceticism and who take as the ideal of human life the poverty and freedom from want of the birds of the forest and the fish of the sea, we can make no reply when they reproach liberalism for its materialistic attitude. We can only ask them to let us go our way undisturbed, just as we do not hinder them from getting to heaven in their own fashion. Let them shut themselves up in their cells, away from men and the world, in peace.

The overwhelming majority of our contemporaries cannot understand the ascetic ideal. But once one rejects the principle of the ascetic conduct of life, one cannot reproach liberalism for aiming at outer well-being.

## 3. Rationalism

Liberalism is usually reproached, besides, for being rationalistic. It wants to regulate everything reasonably and thus fails to recognize that in human affairs great latitude is, and, indeed, must be, given to feelings and to the irrational generally—i.e., to what is unreasonable.

Now liberalism is by no means unaware of the fact that men sometimes act unreasonably. If men always acted reasonably, it would be superfluous to exhort them to be guided by reason. Liberalism does not say that men always act intelligently, but rather that they ought, in their own rightly understood interest, always to act intelligently. And the essence of liberalism is just this, that it wants to have conceded to reason in the sphere of social policy the acceptance that is conceded to it without dispute in all other spheres of human action.

If, having been recommended a reasonable—i.e., hygienic—mode of life by his doctor, someone were to reply: "I know that your advice is reasonable; my feelings, however, forbid me to follow it. I *want* to do what is harmful for my health even though it may be unreasonable," hardly anybody would regard his conduct as commendable. No matter what we undertake to do in life, in order to reach the goal that we have set for ourselves we endeavor to do it reasonably. The person who wants to cross a railroad track will not choose the very moment when a train is passing over the crossing. The person who wants to sew on a button will avoid pricking his finger with the needle. In every sphere of his practical activity man has developed a technique or a technology that indicates how one is to proceed if one does not want to behave in an unreasonable way. It is generally acknowledged that it is desirable for a man to acquire the techniques which he can make use of in life, and a person who enters a field whose techniques he has not mastered is derided as a bungler.

Only in the sphere of social policy, it is thought, should it be otherwise. Here, not reason, but feelings and impulses should decide. The question: How must things be arranged in order to provide good illumination during the hours of darkness? is generally discussed only with reasonable arguments. As soon, however, as the point in the discussion is reached when it is to be decided whether the lighting plant should be managed by private individuals or by the municipality, then reason is no longer considered valid. Here sentiment, world view—in short, unreason—should determine the result. We ask in vain: Why?

The organization of human society according to the pattern most suitable for the attainment of the ends in view is a quite prosaic and matter-of-fact question, not unlike, say, the construction of a railroad or the production of cloth or furniture. National and governmental affairs are, it is true, more important than all other practical questions of human conduct, since the social order furnishes the foundation for everything else, and it is possible for each individual to prosper in the pursuit of his ends only in a society propitious for their attainment. But however lofty may be the sphere in which political and social questions are placed, they still refer to matters that are subject to human control and must consequently be judged according to the canons of human reason. In such matters, no less than in all our other mundane affairs, mysticism is only an evil. Our powers of comprehension are very limited. We cannot hope ever to discover the ultimate and most profound secrets of the universe. But the fact that we can never fathom the meaning and purpose of our existence does not hinder us from taking precautions to avoid contagious diseases or from making use of the appropriate means to feed and clothe ourselves, nor should it deter us from organizing society in such a way that the earthly goals for which we strive can be most effectually attained. Even the state and the legal system, the government and its administration are not too lofty, too good, too grand, for us to bring them within the range of rational deliberation. Problems of social policy are problems of social technology, and their solution must be sought in the same ways and by the same means that are at our disposal in the solution of other technical problems: by rational reflection and by examination of the given conditions. All that man is and all that raises him above the animals he owes to his reason. Why should he forgo the use of reason just in the sphere of social policy and trust to vague and obscure feelings and impulses?

## 4. The Aim of Liberalism

There is a widespread opinion that liberalism is distinguished from other political movements by the fact that it places the interests of a part of society—the propertied classes, the capitalists, the entrepreneurs—above the interests of the other classes. This assertion is completely mistaken. Liberalism has always had in view the good of the whole, not that of any special group. It was this that the English utilitarians meant to express—although, it is true, not very aptly—in their famous formula, "the greatest happiness of the greatest number." Historically, liberalism was the first political movement that aimed at promoting the welfare of all, not that of special groups. Liberalism is distinguished from socialism, which likewise professes to strive for the good of all, not by the goal at which it aims, but by the means that it chooses to attain that goal.

If it is maintained that the consequence of a liberal policy is or must be to favor the special interests of certain strata of society, this is still a question that allows of discussion. It is one of the tasks of the present work to show that such a reproach is in no way justified. But one cannot, from the very outset, impute unfairness to the person who raises it; though we consider his opinion incorrect, it could very well be advanced in the best of faith. In any case, whoever attacks liberalism in this way concedes that its intentions are disinterested and that it wants nothing but what it says it wants.

Quite different are those critics of liberalism who reproach it for wanting to promote, not the general welfare, but only the special interests of certain classes. Such critics are both unfair and ignorant. By choosing this mode of attack, they show that they are inwardly well aware of the weakness of their own case. They snatch at poisoned weapons because they cannot otherwise hope for success.

If a doctor shows a patient who craves food detrimental to his health the perversity of his desire, no one will be so foolish as to say: "The doctor does not care for the good of the patient; whoever wishes the patient well must not grudge him the enjoyment of relishing such delicious food." Everyone will understand that the doctor advises the patient to forgo the pleasure that the enjoyment of the harmful food affords solely in order to avoid injuring his health. But as soon as the matter concerns social policy, one is prone to consider it quite differently. When the liberal advises against certain popular measures because he expects harmful consequences from them, he is censured as an enemy of the people, and praise is heaped on the demagogues who, without consideration of the harm that will follow, recommend what seems to be expedient for the moment.

Reasonable action is distinguished from unreasonable action by the fact that it involves provisional sacrifices. The latter are only apparent sacrifices, since they are outweighed by the favorable consequences that later ensue. The person who avoids tasty but unwholesome food makes merely a provisional, a seeming sacrifice. The outcome—the nonoccurrence of injury to his health —shows that he has not lost, but gained. To act in this way, however, requires insight into the consequences of one's action. The demagogue takes advantage of this fact. He opposes the liberal, who calls for provisional and merely apparent sacrifices, and denounces him as a hard-hearted enemy of the people, meanwhile setting himself up as a friend of humanity. In supporting the measures he advocates, he knows well how to touch the hearts of his hearers and to move them to tears with allusions to want and misery.

Antiliberal policy is a policy of capital consumption. It recommends that the present be more abundantly provided for at the expense of the future. It is in exactly the same case as the patient of whom we have spoken. In both instances a relatively grievous disadvantage in the future stands in opposition to a relatively abundant momentary gratification. To talk, in such a case, as if the question were one of hard-heartedness versus philanthropy is downright dishonest and untruthful. It is not only the common run of politicians and the press of the antiliberal parties that are open to such a reproach. Almost all the writers of the school of *Sozialpolitik* have made use of this underhanded mode of combat.

That there is want and misery in the world is not, as the average newspaper reader, in his dullness, is only too prone to believe, an argument against liberalism. It is precisely want and misery that liberalism seeks to abolish, and it considers the means that it proposes the only suitable ones for the achievement of this end. Let whoever thinks that he knows a better, or even a different, means to this end adduce the proof. The assertion that the liberals do not strive for the good of all members of society, but only for that of special groups, is in no way a substitute for this proof.

The fact that there is want and misery would not constitute an argument against liberalism even if the world today followed a liberal policy. It would always be an open question whether still more want and misery might not prevail if other policies had been followed. In view of all the ways in which the functioning of the institution of private property is curbed and hindered in every quarter today by antiliberal policies, it is manifestly quite absurd to seek to infer anything against the correctness of liberal principles from the fact that economic conditions are not, at present, all that one could wish. In order to appreciate what liberalism and capitalism have accomplished, one should compare conditions as they are at present with those of the Middle Ages or of the first centuries of the modern era. What liberalism and capitalism could have accomplished had they been allowed free rein can be inferred only from theoretical considerations.

## 5. *Liberalism and Capitalism*

A society in which liberal principles are put into effect is usually called a capitalist society, and the condition of that society, capitalism. Since the economic policy of liberalism has everywhere been only more or less closely approximated in practice, conditions as they are in the world today provide us with but an imperfect idea of the meaning and possible accomplishments of capitalism in full flower. Nevertheless, one is altogether justified in calling our age the age of capitalism, because all that has created the wealth of our time can be traced back to capitalist institutions. It is thanks to those liberal ideas that still remain alive in our society, to what yet survives in it of the capitalist system, that the great mass of our contemporaries can enjoy a standard of living far above that which just a few generations ago was possible only to the rich and especially privileged.

To be sure, in the customary rhetoric of the demagogues these facts are represented quite differently. To listen to them, one would think that all progress in the techniques of production redounds to the exclusive benefit of a favored few, while the masses sink ever more deeply into misery. However, it requires only a moment's reflection to realize that the fruits of all technological and industrial innovations make for an improvement in the satisfaction of the wants of the great masses. All big industries that produce consumers' goods work directly for their benefit; all industries that produce machines and half-finished products work for them indirectly. The great industrial developments of the last decades, like those of the eighteenth century that are designated by the not altogether happily chosen phrase, "the Industrial Revolution," have resulted, above all, in a better satisfaction of the needs of the masses. The development of the clothing industry, the mechanization of shoe production, and improvements in the processing and distribution of foodstuffs have, by their very nature, benefited the widest public. It is thanks to these industries that the masses today are far better clothed and fed than ever before. However, mass production provides not only for food, shelter, and clothing, but also for other requirements of the multitude. The press serves the masses quite as much as the motion picture industry, and even the theater and similar strongholds of the arts are daily becoming more and more places of mass entertainment.

Nevertheless, as a result of the zealous propaganda of the antiliberal parties, which twists the facts the other way round, people today have come to associate the ideas of liberalism and capitalism with the image of a world plunged into ever increasing misery and poverty. To be sure, no amount of depreciatory propaganda could ever succeed, as the demagogues had hoped, in giving the words "liberal" and "liberalism" a completely pejorative connotation. In the last analysis, it is not possible to brush aside the fact that, in spite of all the efforts of antiliberal propaganda, there is something in these expressions that suggests what every normal person feels when he hears the word "freedom." Antiliberal propaganda, therefore, avoids mentioning the word "liberalism" too often and prefers the infamies that it attributes to the liberal system to be associated with the term "capitalism." That word brings to mind a flint-hearted capitalist, who thinks of nothing but his own enrichment, even if that is possible only through the exploitation of his fellow men.

It hardly occurs to anyone, when he forms his notion of a capitalist, that a social order organized on genuinely liberal principles is so constituted as to leave the entrepreneurs and the capitalists only one way to wealth, viz., by better providing their fellow men with what they themselves think they need. Instead of speaking of capitalism in connection with the prodigious improvement in the standard of living of the masses, antiliberal propaganda mentions capitalism only in referring to those phenomena whose emergence was made possible solely because of the restraints that were imposed upon liberalism. No reference is made to the fact that capitalism has placed a delectable luxury as well as a food, in the form of sugar, at the disposal of the great masses. Capitalism is mentioned in connection with sugar only when the price of sugar in a country is raised above the world market price by a cartel. As if such a development were even conceivable in a social order in which liberal principles were put into effect! In a country with a liberal regime, in which there are no tariffs, cartels capable of driving the price of a commodity above the world market price would be quite unthinkable.

The links in the chain of reasoning by which antiliberal demagogy succeeds in laying upon liberalism and capitalism the blame for all the excesses and evil consequences of antiliberal policies are as follows: One starts from the assumption that liberal principles aim at promoting the interests of the capitalists and entrepreneurs at the expense of the interests of the rest of the population and that liberalism is a policy that favors the rich over the poor. Then one observes that many entrepreneurs and capitalists, under certain conditions, advocate protective tariffs, and still others—the armaments manufacturers—support a policy of "national preparedness"; and, out of hand, one jumps to the conclusion that these must be "capitalistic" policies.

In fact, however, the case is quite otherwise. Liberalism is not a policy in the interest of any particular group, but a policy in the interest of all mankind. It is, therefore, incorrect to assert that the entrepreneurs and capitalists have any *special* interest in supporting liberalism. Their interest in championing the liberal program is exactly the same as that of everyone else. There may be individual cases in which some entrepreneurs or capitalists cloak their special interests in the program of liberalism; but opposed to these are always the special interests of other entrepreneurs or capitalists. The matter is not quite so simple as those who everywhere scent "interests" and "interested parties" imagine. That a nation imposes a tariff on iron, for example, cannot "simply" be explained by the fact that this benefits the iron magnates. There are also persons with opposing interests in the country, even among the entrepreneurs; and, in any case, the beneficiaries of the tariff on iron are a steadily diminishing minority. Nor can bribery be the explanation, for the people bribed can likewise be only a minority; and, besides, why does only one group, the protectionists, do the bribing, and not their opponents, the freetraders?

The fact is that the ideology that makes the protective tariff possible is created neither by the "interested parties" nor by those bribed by them, but by the ideologists, who give the world the ideas that direct the course of all human affairs. In our age, in which antiliberal ideas prevail, virtually everyone thinks accordingly, just as, a hundred years ago, most people thought in terms of the then prevailing liberal ideology. If many entrepreneurs today advocate protective tariffs, this is nothing more than the form that antiliberalism takes in their case. It has nothing to do with liberalism.

### 6. *The Psychological Roots of Antiliberalism*

It cannot be the task of this book to discuss the problem of social cooperation otherwise than with rational arguments. But the root of the opposition to liberalism cannot be reached by resort to the method of reason. This opposition does not stem from the reason, but from a pathological mental attitude—from resentment and from a neurasthenic condition that one might call a Fourier complex, after the French socialist of that name.

Concerning resentment and envious malevolence little need be said. Resentment is at work when one so hates somebody for his more favorable circumstances that one is prepared to bear heavy losses if only the hated one might also come to harm. Many of those who attack capitalism know very well that their situation under any other economic system will be less favorable. Nevertheless, with full knowledge of this fact, they advocate a reform, e.g., socialism, because they hope that the rich, whom they envy, will also suffer under it. Time and again one hears socialists say that even material want will be easier to bear in a socialist society because people will realize that no one is better off than his neighbor.

At all events, resentment can still be dealt with by rational arguments. It is, after all, not too difficult to make clear to a person who is filled with resentment that the important thing for him cannot be to worsen the position of his better situated fellow men, but to improve his own.

The Fourier complex is much harder to combat. What is involved in this case is a serious disease of the nervous system, a neurosis, which is more properly the concern of the psychologist than of the legislator. Yet it cannot be neglected in investigating the problems of modern society. Unfortunately, medical men have hitherto scarcely concerned themselves with the problems presented by the Fourier complex. Indeed, they have hardly been noticed even by Freud, the great master of psychology, or by his followers in their theory of neurosis, though it is to psycho-analysis that we are indebted for having opened up the path that alone leads to a coherent and systematic understanding of mental disorders of this kind.

Scarcely one person in a million succeeds in fulfilling his life's ambition. The upshot of one's labors, even if one is favored by fortune, remains far inferior to what the wistful daydreams of youth allowed one to hope for. Plans and desires are shattered on a thousand obstacles, and one's powers prove too weak to achieve the goals on which one has set one's heart. The failure of his hopes, the frustration of his schemes, his own inadequacy in the face of the tasks that he has set himself—these constitute every man's most deeply painful experience. They are, indeed, the common lot of man.

There are two ways in which man can react to this experience. One way is indicated by the practical wisdom of Goethe:

> Dost thou fancy that I should hate life,
> Should flee to the wilderness,
> Because not all my budding dreams have
>     blossomed?

his Prometheus cries. And Faust recognizes at the "highest moment" that "the last word of wisdom" is:

No man deserves his freedom or his life
Who does not daily win them anew.

Such a will and such a spirit cannot be vanquished by any earthly misfortune. He who accepts life for what it is and never allows himself to be overwhelmed by it does not need to seek refuge for his crushed self-confidence in the solace of a "saving lie." If the longed-for success is not forthcoming, if the vicissitudes of fate destroy in the twinkling of an eye what had to be painstakingly built up by years of hard work, then he simply multiplies his exertions. He can look disaster in the eye without despairing.

The neurotic cannot endure life in its real form. It is too raw for him, too coarse, too common. To render it bearable he does not, like the healthy man, have the heart to "carry on in spite of everything." That would not be in keeping with his weakness. Instead, he takes refuge in a delusion. A delusion is, according to Freud, "itself something desired, a kind of consolation"; it is characterized by its "resistance to attack by logic and reality." It by no means suffices, therefore, to seek to talk the patient out of his delusion by conclusive demonstrations of its absurdity. In order to recuperate, the patient himself must overcome it. He must learn to understand why he does not want to face the truth and why he takes refuge in delusions.

Only the theory of neurosis can explain the success enjoyed by Fourierism, the mad product of a seriously deranged brain. This is not the place to adduce evidence of Fourier's psychosis by quoting passages from his writings. Such descriptions are of interest only to the psychiatrist and, perhaps, also to people who derive a certain pleasure from reading the productions of a lewd phantasy. But the fact is that Marxism, when it is obliged to leave the field of pompous dialectical rhetoric and the derision and defamation of its opponents and to make a few meager remarks pertinent to the issue, never has anything different to advance from what Fourier, the "utopian," had to offer.

Marxism is likewise unable to construct a picture of a socialist society without making two assumptions already made by Fourier that contradict all experience and all reason. On the one hand, it assumes that the "material substratum" of production, which is "already present in nature without the need of productive effort on the part of man," stands at our disposal in such abundance that it need not be economized; hence the faith of Marxism in a "practically limitless increase in production." On the other hand, it assumes that in a socialist community work will change from "a burden into a pleasure"—indeed, that it will become "the primary necessity of life." Where a superfluity of all goods abounds and work is a pleasure, it is, doubtless, an easy matter to establish a land of Cockaigne.

Marxism believes that from the height of its "scientific socialism" it is entitled to look down with contempt on romanticism and romantics. But in reality its own procedure is no different from theirs. Instead of removing the impediments that stand in the way of the realization of its desires, it too prefers to let all obstacles simply fade away in the mists of phantasy.

In the life of the neurotic the "saving lie" has a double function. It not only consoles him for past failure, but holds out the prospect of future success. In the case of social failure, which alone concerns us here, the consolation consists in the belief that one's inability to attain the lofty goals to which one has aspired is not to be ascribed to one's own inadequacy, but to the defectiveness of the social order. The malcontent expects from the overthrow of the latter the success that the existing system has withheld from him. Consequently, it is entirely futile to try to make clear to him that the utopia he dreams of is not feasible and that the only foundation possible for a society organized on the principle of the division of labor is private ownership of the means of production. The neurotic clings to his "saving lie," and when he must make the choice of renouncing either it or logic, he prefers to sacrifice logic. For life would be unbearable for him without the consolation that he finds in the idea of socialism. It tells him that not he himself, but the world, is at fault for having caused his failure; and this conviction raises his depressed self-confidence and liberates him from a tormenting feeling of inferiority.

Just as the devout Christian could more easily endure the misfortune that befell him on earth because he hoped for a continuation of personal existence in another, better world, where those who on earth had been first would be last and the last would be first; so, for modern man, socialism has become an elixir against earthly adversity. But whereas the belief in immortality, in a recompense in the hereafter, and in resurrection formed an incentive to virtuous conduct in this life, the effect of the socialist promise is quite different. It imposes no other duty than that of giving political support to the party of socialism; but at the same time it raises expectations and demands.

This being the character of the socialist dream, it is understandable that every one of the partisans of socialism expects from it precisely what has so far been denied to him. Socialist authors promise not only wealth for all, but also happiness in love for everybody, the full physical and spiritual development of each individual, the unfolding of great artistic and scientific talents in all men, etc. Only recently Trotsky stated in one of his writings that in the socialist society "the average human type will rise to the heights of an Aristotle, a Goethe, or a Marx. And above this ridge new peaks will rise." [1] The socialist paradise will be the kingdom of perfection, populated by completely happy supermen. All socialist literature is full of such nonsense. But it is just this nonsense that wins it the most supporters.

One cannot send every person suffering from a Fourier complex to the doctor for psychoanalytic treatment; the number of those afflicted with it is far too great. No other remedy is possible in this case than the treatment of the illness by the patient himself. Through self-knowledge he must learn to endure his lot in life without looking for a scapegoat on which he can lay all the blame, and he must endeavor to grasp the fundamental laws of social cooperation.

# 1

# The Foundations of Liberal Policy

## 1. *Property*

Human society is an association of persons for cooperative action. As against the isolated action of individuals, cooperative action on the basis of the principle of the division of labor has the advantage of greater productivity. If a number of men work in cooperation in accordance with the principle of the division of labor, they will produce (other things being equal) not only as much as the sum of what they would have produced by working as self-sufficient individuals, but considerably more. All human civilization is founded on this fact. It is by virtue of the division of labor that man is distinguished from the animals. It is the division of labor that has made feeble man, far inferior to most animals in physical strength, the lord of the earth and the creator of the marvels of technology. In the absence of the division of labor, we would not be in any respect further advanced today than our ancestors of a thousand or ten thousand years ago.

Human labor by itself is not capable of increasing our well-being. In order to be fruitful, it must be applied to the materials and resources of the earth that Nature has placed at our disposal. Land, with all the substances and powers resident within it, and human labor constitute the two factors of production from whose purposeful cooperation proceed all the commodities that serve for the satisfaction of our outer needs. In order to produce, one must deploy labor and the material factors of production, including not only the raw materials and resources placed at our disposal by Nature and mostly found in the earth, but also the intermediate products already fabricated of these primary natural factors of production by previously performed human labor. In the language of economics we distinguish, accordingly, three factors of production: labor, land, and capital. By land is to be understood everything that Nature places at our disposal in the way of substances and powers on, under, and above the surface of the earth, in the water, and in the air; by capital goods, all the intermediate goods produced from land with the help of human labor that are made to serve further production, such as machines, tools, half-manufactured articles of all kinds, etc.

Now we wish to consider two different systems of human cooperation under the division of labor—one based on private ownership of the means of production, and the other based on communal ownership of the means of production. The latter is called socialism or communism; the former, liberalism or also (ever since it created in the nineteenth century a division of labor encompassing the whole world) capitalism. The liberals maintain that the only workable system of human cooperation in a society based on the division of labor is private ownership of the means of production. They contend that socialism as a completely comprehensive system encompassing all the means of production is unworkable and that the application of the socialist principle to a part of the means of production, though not, of course, impossible, leads to a reduction in the productivity of labor, so that, far from creating greater wealth, it must, on the contrary, have the effect of diminishing wealth.

The program of liberalism, therefore, if condensed into a single word, would have to read: *property*, that is, private ownership of the means of production (for in regard to commodities ready for consumption, private ownership is a matter of course and is not disputed even by the socialists and communists). All the other demands of liberalism result from this fundamental demand.

Side by side with the word "property" in the program of liberalism one may quite appropriately place the words "freedom" and "peace." This is not because the older program of liberalism generally placed them there. We have already said that the program of present-day liberalism has outgrown that of the older liberalism, that it is based on a deeper and better insight into interrelationships, since it can reap the benefit of the advances that science has made in the last decades. Freedom and peace have been placed in the forefront of the program of liberalism, not because many of the older liberals regarded them as coordinate with the fundamental principle of liberalism itself, rather than as merely a necessary consequence following from the one fundamental principle of the private ownership of the means of production; but solely because freedom and peace have come under especially violent attack from the opponents of liberalism, and liberals have not wanted to give the appearance, through the omission of these principles, that they in any way acknowledged the justness of the objections raised against them.

## 2. Freedom

The idea of freedom has become so ingrained in all of us that for a long time no one dared to call it into question. People were accustomed always to speaking of freedom only with the greatest of reverence; it remained for Lenin to call it a "bourgeois prejudice." Although the fact is often forgotten today, all this is an achievement of liberalism. The very name of liberalism is derived from freedom, and the name of the party in opposition to the liberals (both designations arose in the Spanish constitutional struggles of the first decades of the nineteenth century) was originally the "servile."

Before the rise of liberalism even high-minded philosophers, founders of religions, clerics animated by the best of intentions, and statesmen who genuinely loved their people, viewed the thralldom of a part of the human race as a just, generally useful, and downright beneficial institution. Some men and peoples are, it was thought, destined by nature for freedom, and others for bondage. And it was not only the masters who thought so, but the greater number of the slaves as well. They put up with their servitude, not only because they had to yield to the superior force of the masters, but also because they found some good in it: the slave is relieved of concern for securing his daily bread, for the master is obliged to provide him with the necessities of life. When liberalism set out, in the eighteenth and the first half of the nineteenth century, to abolish the serfdom and subjection of the peasant population in Europe and the slavery of the Negroes in the overseas colonies, not a few sincere humanitarians declared themselves in opposition. Unfree laborers are used to their bondage and do not feel it as an evil. They are not ready for freedom and would not know how to make use of it. The discontinuation of the master's care would be very harmful to them. They would not be capable of managing their affairs in such a way as always to provide more than just the bare necessities of life, and they would soon fall into want and misery. Emancipation would thus not only fail to gain for them anything of real value, but would seriously impair their material well-being.

What was astonishing was that one could hear these views expressed even by many of the slaves whom one questioned. In order to counter such opinions, many liberals believed it necessary to represent as the general rule and even on occasion to depict in an exaggerated manner the exceptional cases in which serfs and slaves had been cruelly abused. But these excesses were by no means the rule. There were, of course, isolated instances of abuse, and the fact that there were such cases was an additional reason for the abolition of this system. As a rule, however, the treatment of bondsmen by their masters was humane and mild.

When those who recommended the abolition of involuntary servitude on general humanitarian grounds were told that the retention of the system was also in the interest of the enslaved, they knew of nothing to say in rejoinder. For against this objection in favor of slavery there is only *one* argument that can and did refute all others—namely, that free labor is incomparably more productive than slave labor. The slave has no interest in exerting himself fully. He works only as much and as zealously as is necessary to escape the punishment attaching to failure to perform the minimum. The free worker, on the other hand, knows that the more his labor accomplishes, the more he will be paid. He exerts himself to the full in order to raise his income. One has only to compare the demands placed on the worker by the tending of a modern tractor with the relatively small expenditure of intelligence, strength, and industry that just two generations ago was deemed sufficient for the enthralled ploughmen of Russia. Only free labor can accomplish what must be demanded of the modern industrial worker.

Muddleheaded babblers may therefore argue interminably over whether all men are destined for freedom and are as yet ready for it. They may go on contending that there are races and peoples for whom Nature has prescribed a life of servitude and that the master races have the duty of keeping the rest of mankind in bondage. The liberal will not oppose their arguments in any way because his reasoning in favor of freedom for all, without distinction, is of an entirely different kind. We liberals do not assert that God or Nature meant all men to be free, because we are not instructed in the designs of God and of Nature, and we avoid, on principle, drawing God and Nature into a dispute over mundane questions. What we maintain is only that a system based on freedom for all workers warrants the greatest productivity of human labor and is therefore in the interest of all the inhabitants of the earth. We attack involuntary servitude, not in spite of the fact that it is advantageous to the "masters," but because we are convinced that, in the last analysis, it hurts the interests of all members of human society, including the "masters." If mankind had adhered to the practice of keeping the whole or even a part of the labor force in bondage, the magnificent economic developments of the last hundred and fifty years would not have been possible. We would have no railroads, no automobiles, no airplanes, no steamships, no electric light and power, no chemical industry, just as the ancient Greeks and Romans, with all their genius, were without these things. It suffices merely to mention this for everyone to realize that even the former masters of slaves or serfs have every reason to be satisfied with the course of events after the abolition of involuntary servitude. The European worker today lives under more favorable and more agreeable outward circumstances than the pharaoh of Egypt once did, in spite of the fact that the pharaoh commanded thousands of slaves, while the worker has nothing to depend on but the strength and skill of his hands. If a nabob of yore could be placed in the circumstances in which a common man lives today, he would declare without hesitation that his life had been a beggarly one in comparison with the life that even a man of moderate means can lead at present.

This is the fruit of free labor. It is able to create more wealth for everyone than slave labor once provided for the masters.

## 3. Peace

There are high-minded men who detest war because it brings death and suffering. However much one may admire their humanitarianism, their argument against war, in being based on philanthropic grounds, seems to lose much or all of its force when we consider the statements of the supporters and proponents of war. The latter by no means deny that war brings with it pain and sorrow. Nevertheless, they believe it is through war and war alone that mankind is able to make progress. War is the father of all things, said a Greek philosopher, and thousands have repeated it after him. Man degenerates in time of peace. Only war awakens in him slumbering talents and powers and imbues him with sublime ideals. If war were to be abolished, mankind would decay into indolence and stagnation.

It is difficult or even impossible to refute this line of reasoning on the part of the advocates of war if the only objection to war that one can think of is that it demands sacrifices. For the proponents of war are of the opinion that these sacrifices are not made in vain and that they are well worth making. If it were really true that war is the father of all things, then the human sacrifices it requires would be necessary to further the general welfare and the progress of humanity. One might lament the sacrifices, one might even strive to reduce their number, but one would not be warranted in wanting to abolish war and to bring about eternal peace.

The liberal critique of the argument in favor of war is fundamentally different from that of the humanitarians. It starts from the premise that not war, but peace, is the father of all things. What alone enables mankind to advance and distinguishes man from the animals is social cooperation. It is labor alone that is productive: it creates wealth and therewith lays the outward foundations for the inward flowering of man. War only destroys; it cannot create. War, carnage, destruction, and devastation we have in common with the predatory beasts of the jungle; constructive labor is our distinctively human characteristic. The liberal abhors war, not, like the humanitarian, in spite of the fact that it has beneficial consequences, but because it has only harmful ones.

The peace-loving humanitarian approaches the mighty potentate and addresses him thus: "Do not make war, even though you have the prospect of furthering your own welfare by a victory. Be noble and magnanimous and renounce the tempting victory even if it means a sacrifice for you and the loss of an advantage." The liberal thinks otherwise. He is convinced that victorious war is an evil even for the victor, that peace is always better than war. He demands no sacrifice from the stronger, but only that he should come to realize where his true interests lie and should learn to understand that peace is for him, the stronger, just as advantageous as it is for the weaker.

When a peace-loving nation is attacked by a bellicose enemy, it must offer resistance and do everything to ward off the onslaught. Heroic deeds performed in such a war by those fighting for their freedom and their lives are entirely praiseworthy, and one rightly extols the manliness and courage of such fighters. Here daring, intrepidity, and contempt for death are praiseworthy because they are in the service of a good end. But people have made the mistake of representing these soldierly virtues as absolute virtues, as qualities good in and for themselves, without consideration of the end they serve. Whoever holds this opinion must, to be consistent, likewise acknowledge as noble virtues the daring, intrepidity, and contempt for death of the robber. In fact, however, there is nothing good or bad in and of itself. Human actions become good or bad only through the end that they serve and the consequences they entail. Even Leonidas would not be worthy of the esteem in which we hold him if he had fallen, not as the defender of his homeland, but as the leader of an invading army intent on robbing a peaceful people of its freedom and possessions.

How harmful war is to the development of human civilization becomes clearly apparent once one understands the advantages derived from the division of labor. The division of labor turns the self-sufficient individual into the ζῷον πολιτικόν dependent on his fellow men, the social animal of which Aristotle spoke. Hostilities between one animal and another, or between one savage and another, in no way alter the economic basis of their existence. The matter is quite different when a quarrel that has to be decided by an appeal to arms breaks out among the members of a community in which labor is divided. In such a society each individual has a specialized function; no one is any longer in a position to live independently, because all have need of one another's aid and support. Self-sufficient farmers, who produce on their own farms everything that they and their families need, can make war on one another. But when a village divides into factions, with the smith on one side and the shoemaker on the other, one faction will have to suffer from want of shoes, and the other from want of tools and weapons. Civil war destroys the division of labor inasmuch as it compels each group to content itself with the labor of its own adherents.

If the possibility of such hostilities had been considered likely in the first place, the division of labor would never have been allowed to develop to the point where, in case a fight really did break out, one would have to suffer privation. The progressive intensification of the division of labor is possible only in a society in which there is an assurance of lasting peace. Only under the shelter of such security can the division of labor develop. In the absence of this prerequisite, the division of labor does not extend beyond the limits of the village or even of the individual household. The division of labor between town and country—with the peasants of the surrounding villages furnishing grain, cattle, milk, and butter to the town in exchange for the manufactured products of the townsfolk—already presupposes that peace is assured at least within the region in question. If the division of labor is to embrace a whole nation, civil war must lie outside the realm of possibility; if it is to encompass the whole world, lasting peace among nations must be assured.

Everyone today would regard it as utterly senseless for a modern metropolis like London or Berlin to prepare to make war on the inhabitants of the adjacent countryside. Yet for many centuries the towns of Europe kept this possibility in mind and made economic provision for it. There were towns whose fortifications were, from the very beginning, so constructed that in case of need they could hold out for a while by keeping cattle and growing grain within the town walls.

At the beginning of the nineteenth century by far the greater part of the inhabited world was still divided into a number of economic regions that were, by and large, self-sufficient. Even in the more highly developed areas of Europe, the needs of a region were met, for the most part, by the production of the region itself. Trade that went beyond the narrow confines of the immediate vicinity was relatively insignificant and comprised, by and large, only such commodities as could not be produced in the area itself because of climatic conditions. In by far the greater part of the world, however, the production of the village itself supplied almost all the needs of its inhabitants. For these villagers, a disturbance in trade relations caused by war did not generally mean any impairment of their economic well-being. But even the inhabitants of the more advanced countries of Europe did not suffer very severely in time of war. If the Continental System, which Napoleon I imposed on Europe in order to exclude from the continent English goods and those coming from across the ocean only by way of England, had been enforced even more rigorously than it was, it would have still inflicted on the inhabitants of the continent hardly any appreciable privations. They would, of course, have had to do without coffee and sugar, cotton and cotton goods, spices, and many rare kinds of wood; but all these things then played only a subordinate role in the households of the great masses.

The development of a complex network of international economic relations is a product of nineteenth-century liberalism and capitalism. They alone made possible the extensive specialization of modern production with its concomitant improvement in technology. In order to provide the family of an English worker with all it consumes and desires, every nation of the five continents cooperates. Tea for the breakfast table is provided by Japan or Ceylon, coffee by Brazil or Java, sugar by the West Indies, meat by Australia or Argentina, cotton from America or Egypt, hides for leather from India or Russia, and so on. And in exchange for these things, English goods go to all parts of the world, to the most remote and out-of-the-way villages and farmsteads. This development was possible and conceivable only because, with the triumph of liberal principles, people no longer took seriously the idea that a great war could ever again break out. In the golden age of liberalism, war among members of the white race was generally considered a thing of the past.

But events have turned out quite differently. Liberal ideas and programs were supplanted by socialism, nationalism, protectionism, imperialism, etatism, and militarism. Whereas Kant and Von Humboldt, Bentham and Cobden had sung the praises of eternal peace, the spokesmen of a later age never tired of extolling war, both civil and international. And their success came only all too soon. The result was the World War, which has given our age a kind of object lesson on the incompatibility between war and the division of labor.

## 4. *Equality*

Nowhere is the difference between the reasoning of the older liberalism and that of neoliberalism clearer and easier to demonstrate than in their treatment of the problem of equality. The liberals of the eighteenth century, guided by the ideas of natural law and of the Enlightenment, demanded for everyone equality of political and civil rights because they assumed that all men are equal. God created all men equal, endowing them with fundamentally the same capabilities and talents, breathing into all of them the breath of His spirit. All distinctions between men are only artificial, the product of social, human—that is to say, transitory—institutions. What is imperishable in man—his spirit —is undoubtedly the same in rich and poor, noble and commoner, white and colored.

Nothing, however, is as ill-founded as the assertion of the alleged equality of all members of the human race. Men are altogether unequal. Even between brothers there exist the most marked differences in physical and mental attributes. Nature never repeats itself in its creations; it produces nothing by the dozen, nor are its products standardized. Each man who leaves her workshop bears the imprint of the individual, the unique, the never-to-recur. Men are not equal, and the demand for equality under the law can by no means be grounded in the contention that equal treatment is due to equals.

There are two distinct reasons why all men should receive equal treatment under the law. One was already mentioned when we analyzed the objections to involuntary servitude. In order for human labor to realize its highest attainable productivity, the worker must be free, because only the free worker, enjoying in the form of wages the fruits of his own industry, will exert himself to the full. The second consideration in favor of the equality of all men under the law is the maintenance of social peace. It has already been pointed out that every disturbance of the peaceful development of the division of labor must be avoided. But it is well-nigh impossible to preserve lasting peace in a society in which the rights and duties of the respective classes are different. Whoever denies rights to a part of the population must always be prepared for a united attack by the disenfranchised on the privileged. Class privileges must disappear so that the conflict over them may cease.

It is therefore quite unjustifiable to find fault with the manner in which liberalism put into effect its postulate of equality, on the ground that what it created was *only* equality before the law, and not real equality. All human power would be insufficient to make men really equal. Men are and will always remain unequal. It is sober considerations of utility such as those we have here presented that constitute the argument in favor of the equality of all men under the law. Liberalism never aimed at anything more than this, nor could it ask for anything more. It is beyond human power to make a Negro white. But the Negro can be granted the same rights as the white man and thereby offered the possibility of earning as much if he produces as much.

But, the socialists say, it is not enough to make men equal before the law. In order to make them really equal, one must also allot them the same income. It is not enough to abolish privileges of birth and of rank. One must finish the job and do away with the greatest and most important privilege of all, namely, that which is accorded by private property. Only then will the liberal program be completely realized, and a consistent liberalism thus leads ultimately to socialism, to the abolition of private ownership of the means of production.

Privilege is an institutional arrangement favoring some individuals or a certain group at the expense of the rest. The privilege exists, although it harms some—perhaps the majority— and benefits no one except those for whose advantage it was created. In the feudal order of the Middle Ages certain lords had the hereditary right to hold a judgeship. They were judges because they had inherited the position, regardless of whether they possessed the abilities and qualities of character that fit a man to be a judge. In their eyes this office was nothing more than a lucrative source of income. Here judgeship was the privilege of a class of noble birth.

If, however, as in modern states, judges are always drawn from the circle of those with legal knowledge and experience, this does not constitute a privilege in favor of lawyers. Preference is given to lawyers, not for their sake, but for the sake of the public welfare, because people are generally of the opinion that a knowledge of jurisprudence is an indispensable prerequisite for holding a judgeship. The question whether a certain institutional arrangement is or is not to be regarded as a privilege granted to a certain group, class, or person is not to be decided by whether or not it is advantageous to that group, class, or person, but according to how beneficial to the general public it is considered to be. The fact that on a ship at sea one man is captain and the rest constitute his crew and are subject to his command is certainly an advantage for the captain. Nevertheless, it is not a privilege of the captain if he possesses the ability to steer the ship between reefs in a storm and thereby to be of service not only to himself, but to the whole crew.

In order to determine whether an institutional arrangement is to be regarded as the special privilege of an individual or of a class, the question one should ask is not whether it benefits this or that individual or class, but only whether it is beneficial to the general public. If we reach the conclusion that only private ownership of the means of production makes possible the prosperous development of human society, it is clear that this is tantamount to saying that private property is not a privilege of the property owner, but a social institution for the good and benefit of all, even though it may at the same time be especially agreeable and advantageous to some.

It is not on behalf of property owners that liberalism favors the preservation of the institution of private property. It is not because the abolition of that institution would violate property rights that the liberals want to preserve it. If they considered the abolition of the institution of private property to be in the general interest, they would advocate that it be abolished, no matter how prejudicial such a policy might be to the interests of property owners. However, the preservation of that institution is in the interest of all strata of society. Even the poor man, who can call nothing his own, lives incomparably better in our society than he would in one that would prove incapable of producing even a fraction of what is produced in our own.

## 5. *The Inequality of Wealth and Income*

What is most criticized in our social order is the inequality in the distribution of wealth and income. There are rich and poor; there are very rich and very poor. The way out is not far to seek: the equal distribution of all wealth.

The first objection to this proposal is that it will not help the situation much because those of moderate means far outnumber the rich, so that each individual could expect from such a distribution only a quite insignificant increment in his standard of living. This is certainly correct, but the argument is not complete. Those who advocate equality of income distribution overlook the most important point, namely, that the total available for distribution, the annual product of social labor, is not independent of the manner in which it is divided. The fact that that product today is as great as it is, is not a natural or technological phenomenon independent of all social conditions, but entirely the result of our social institutions. Only because inequality of wealth is possible in our social order, only because it stimulates everyone to produce as much as he can and at the lowest cost, does mankind today have at its disposal the total annual wealth now available for consumption. Were this incentive to be destroyed, productivity would be so greatly reduced that the portion that an equal distribution would allot to each individual would be far less than what even the poorest receives today.

The inequality of income distribution has, however, still a second function quite as important as the one already mentioned: it makes possible the luxury of the rich.

Many foolish things have been said and written about luxury. Against luxury consumption it has been objected that it is unjust that some should enjoy great abundance while others are in want. This argument seems to have some merit. But it only seems so. For if it can be shown that luxury consumption performs a useful function in the system of social cooperation, then the argument will be proved invalid. This, however, is what we shall seek to demonstrate.

Our defense of luxury consumption is not, of course, the argument that one occasionally hears, that is, that it spreads money among the people. If the rich did not indulge themselves in luxuries, it is said, the poor would have no income. This is simply nonsense. For if there were no luxury consumption, the capital and labor that would otherwise have been applied to the production of luxury goods would produce other goods: articles of mass consumption, necessary articles, instead of "superfluous" ones.

To form a correct conception of the social significance of luxury consumption, one must first of all realize that the concept of luxury is an altogether relative one. Luxury consists in a way of living that stands in sharp contrast to that of the great mass of one's contemporaries. The conception of luxury is, therefore, essentially historical. Many things that seem to us necessities today were once considered as luxuries. When, in the Middle Ages, an aristocratic Byzantine lady who had married a Venetian doge made use of a golden implement, which could be called the forerunner of the fork as we know it today, instead of her fingers, in eating her meals, the Venetians looked on this as a godless luxury, and they thought it only just when the lady was stricken with a dreadful disease; this must be, they supposed, the well-merited punishment of God for such unnatural extravagance. Two or three generations ago even in England an indoor bathroom was considered a luxury; today the home of every English worker of the better type contains one. Thirty-five years ago there were no automobiles; twenty years ago the possession of such a vehicle was the sign of a particularly luxurious mode of living; today in the United States even the worker has his Ford. This is the course of economic history. The luxury of today is the necessity of tomorrow. Every advance first comes into being as the luxury of a few rich people, only to become, after a time, the indispensable necessity taken for granted by everyone. Luxury consumption provides industry with the stimulus to discover and introduce new things. It is one of the dynamic factors in our economy. To it we owe the progressive innovations by which the standard of living of all strata of the population has been gradually raised.

Most of us have no sympathy with the rich idler who spends his life in pleasure without ever doing any work. But even he fulfills a function in the life of the social organism. He sets an example of luxury that awakens in the multitude a consciousness of new needs and gives industry the incentive to fulfill them. There was a time when only the rich could afford the luxury of visiting foreign countries. Schiller never saw the Swiss mountains, which he celebrated in *Wilhelm Tell*, although they bordered on his Swabian homeland. Goethe saw neither Paris nor Vienna nor London. Today, however, hundreds of thousands travel, and soon millions will do so.

## 6. *Private Property and Ethics*

In seeking to demonstrate the social function and necessity of private ownership of the means of production and of the concomitant inequality in the distribution of income and wealth, we are at the same time providing proof of the moral justification for private property and for the capitalist social order based upon it.

Morality consists in the regard for the necessary requirements of social existence that must be demanded of each individual member of society. A man living in isolation has no moral rules to follow. He need have no qualms about doing anything he finds it to his advantage to do, for he does not have to consider whether he is not thereby injuring others. But as a member of society, a man must take into consideration, in everything he does, not only his own immediate advantage, but also the necessity, in every action, of affirming society as such. For the life of the individual in society is possible only by virtue of social cooperation, and every individual would be most seriously harmed if the social organization of life and of production were to break down. In requiring of the individual that he should take society into consideration in all his actions, that he should forgo an action that, while advantageous to him, would be detrimental to social life, society does not demand that he sacrifice himself to the interests of others. For the sacrifice that it imposes is only a provisional one: the renunciation of an immediate and relatively minor advantage in exchange for a much greater ultimate benefit. The continued existence of society as the association of persons working in cooperation and sharing a common way of life is in the interest of every individual. Whoever gives up a momentary advantage in order to avoid imperiling the continued existence of society is sacrificing a lesser gain for a greater one.

The meaning of this regard for the general social interest has frequently been misunderstood. Its moral value was believed to consist in the fact of the sacrifice itself, in the renunciation of an immediate gratification. One refused to see that what is morally valuable is not the sacrifice, but the end served by the sacrifice, and one insisted on ascribing moral value to sacrifice, to renunciation, in and for itself alone. But sacrificing is moral only when it serves a moral end. There is a world of difference between a man who risks his life and property for a good cause and the man who sacrifices them without benefiting society in any way.

Everything that serves to preserve the social order is moral; everything that is detrimental to it is immoral. Accordingly, when we reach the conclusion that an institution is beneficial to society, one can no longer object that it is immoral. There may possibly be a difference of opinion about whether a particular institution is socially beneficial or harmful. But once it has been judged beneficial, one can no longer contend that, for some inexplicable reason, it must be condemned as immoral.

## 7. State and Government

The observance of the moral law is in the ultimate interest of every individual, because everyone benefits from the preservation of social cooperation; yet it imposes on everyone a sacrifice, even though only a provisional one that is more than counterbalanced by a greater gain. To perceive this, however, requires a certain insight into the connection between things, and to conform one's actions in accordance with this perception demands a certain strength of will. Those who lack the perception, or, having the perception, lack the necessary will power to put it to use, are not able to conform to the moral law voluntarily.

The situation here is no different from that involved in the observance of the rules of hygiene that the individual ought to follow in the interest of his own well-being. Someone may give himself over to unwholesome dissipation, such as indulgence in narcotics, whether because he does not know the consequences, or because he considers them less disadvantageous than the renunciation of the momentary pleasure, or because he lacks the requisite will power to adjust his behavior to his knowledge. There are people who consider that society is justified in resorting to coercive measures to set such a person on the right path and to correct anyone whose heedless actions imperil his own life and health. They advocate that alcoholics and drug addicts be forcibly deterred from indulging their vices and compelled to protect their good health.

The question whether compulsion really answers the purpose in such cases we shall reserve for later consideration. What concerns us here is something quite different, namely, the question whether people whose actions endanger the continued existence of society should be compelled to refrain from doing so. The alcoholic and the drug addict harm only themselves by their behavior; the person who violates the rules of morality governing man's life in society harms not only himself, but everyone. Life in society would be quite impossible if the people who desire its continued existence and who conduct themselves accordingly had to forgo the use of force and compulsion against those who are prepared to undermine society by their behavior. A small number of antisocial individuals, i.e., persons who are not willing or able to make the temporary sacrifices that society demands of them, could make all society impossible. Without the application of compulsion and coercion against the enemies of society, there could not be any life in society.

We call the social apparatus of compulsion and coercion that induces people to abide by the rules of life in society, the state; the rules according to which the state proceeds, law; and the organs charged with the responsibility of administering the apparatus of compulsion, government.

There is, to be sure, a sect that believes that one could quite safely dispense with every form of compulsion and base society entirely on the voluntary observance of the moral code. The anarchists consider state, law, and government as superfluous institutions in a social order that would really serve the good of all, and not just the special interests of a privileged few. Only because the present social order is based on private ownership of the means of production is it necessary to resort to compulsion and coercion in its defense. If private property were abolished, then everyone, without exception, would spontaneously observe the rules demanded by social cooperation.

It has already been pointed out that this doctrine is mistaken in so far as it concerns the character of private ownership of the means of production. But even apart from this, it is altogether untenable. The anarchist, rightly enough, does not deny that every form of human cooperation in a society based on the division of labor demands the observance of some rules of conduct that are not always agreeable to the individual, since they impose on him a sacrifice, only temporary, it is true, but, for all that, at least for the moment, painful. But the anarchist is mistaken in assuming that everyone, without exception, will be willing to observe these rules *voluntarily*. There are dyspeptics who, though they know very well that indulgence in a certain food will, after a short time, cause them severe, even scarcely bearable pains, are nevertheless unable to forgo the enjoyment of the delectable dish. Now the interrelationships of life in society are not as easy to trace as the physiological effects of a food, nor do the consequences follow so quickly and, above all, so palpably for the evildoer. Can it, then, be assumed, without falling completely into absurdity, that, in spite of all this, every individual in an anarchist society will have greater foresight and will power than a gluttonous dyspeptic? In an anarchist society is the possibility entirely to be excluded that someone may negligently throw away a lighted match and start a fire or, in a fit of anger, jealousy, or revenge, inflict injury on his fellow man? Anarchism misunderstands the real nature of man. It would be practicable only in a world of angels and saints.

Liberalism is not anarchism, nor has it anything whatsoever to do with anarchism. The liberal understands quite clearly that without resort to compulsion, the existence of society would be endangered and that behind the rules of conduct whose observance is necessary to assure peaceful human cooperation must stand the threat of force if the whole edifice of society is not to be continually at the mercy of any one of its members. One must be in a position to compel the person who will not respect the lives, health, personal freedom, or private property of others to acquiesce in the rules of life in society. This is the function that the liberal doctrine assigns to the state: the protection of property, liberty, and peace.

The German socialist, Ferdinand Lassalle, tried to make the conception of a government limited exclusively to this sphere appear ridiculous by calling the state constituted on the basis of liberal principles the "night-watchman state." But it is difficult to see why the night-watchman state should be any more ridiculous or worse than the state that concerns itself with the preparation of sauerkraut, with the manufacture of trouser buttons, or with the publication of newspapers. In order to understand the impression that Lassalle was seeking to create with this witticism, one must keep in mind that the Germans of his time had not yet forgotten the state of the monarchical despots, with its vast multiplicity of administrative and regulatory functions, and that they were still very much under the influence of the philosophy of Hegel, which had elevated the state to the position of a divine entity. If one looked upon the state, with Hegel, as "the self-conscious moral substance," as the "Universal in and for itself, the rationality of the will," then, of course, one had to view as blasphemous any attempt to limit the function of the state to that of serving as a night watchman.

It is only thus that one can understand how it was possible for people to go so far as to reproach liberalism for its "hostility" or enmity towards the state. If I am of the opinion that it is inexpedient to assign to the government the task of operating railroads, hotels, or mines, I am not an "enemy of the state" any more than I can be called an enemy of sulphuric acid because I am of the opinion that, useful though it may be for many purposes, it is not suitable either for drinking or for washing one's hands.

It is incorrect to represent the attitude of liberalism toward the state by saying that it wishes to restrict the latter's sphere of possible activity or that it abhors, in principle, all activity on the part of the state in relation to economic life. Such an interpretation is altogether out of the question. The stand that liberalism takes in regard to the problem of the function of the state is the necessary consequence of its advocacy of private ownership of the means of production. If one is in favor of the latter, one cannot, of course, also be in favor of communal ownership of the means of production, i.e., of placing them at the disposition of the government rather than of individual owners. Thus, the advocacy of private ownership of the means of production already implies a very severe circumscription of the functions assigned to the state.

The socialists are sometimes wont to reproach liberalism with a lack of consistency. It is, they maintain, illogical to restrict the activity of the state in the economic sphere exclusively to the protection of property. It is difficult to see why, if the state is not to remain completely neutral, its intervention has to be limited to protecting the rights of property owners.

This reproach would be justified only if the opposition of liberalism to all governmental activity in the economic sphere going beyond the protection of property stemmed from an aversion in principle against any activity on the part of the state. But that is by no means the case. The reason why liberalism opposes a further extension of the sphere of governmental activity is precisely that this would, in effect, abolish private ownership of the means of production. And in private property the liberal sees the principle most suitable for the organization of man's life in society.

## 8. Democracy

Liberalism is therefore far from disputing the necessity of a machinery of state, a system of law, and a government. It is a grave misunderstanding to associate it in any way with the idea of anarchism. For the liberal, the state is an absolute necessity, since the most important tasks are incumbent upon it: the protection not only of private property, but also of peace, for in the absence of the latter the full benefits of private property cannot be reaped.

These considerations alone suffice to determine the conditions that a state must fulfill in order to correspond to the liberal ideal. It must not only be able to protect private property; it must also be so constituted that the smooth and peaceful course of its development is never interrupted by civil wars, revolutions, or insurrections.

Many people are still haunted by the idea, which dates back to the preliberal era, that a certain nobility and dignity attaches to the exercise of governmental functions. Up to very recently public officials in Germany enjoyed, and indeed still enjoy even today, a prestige that has made the most highly respected career that of a civil servant. The social esteem in which a young "assessor" * or lieutenant is held far exceeds that of a businessman or an attorney grown old in honest labor. Writers, scholars, and artists whose fame and glory have spread far beyond Germany enjoy in their own homeland only the respect corresponding to the often rather modest rank they occupied in the bureaucratic hierarchy.

There is no rational basis for this overestimation of the activities carried on in the offices of the administrative authorities. It is a form of atavism, a vestige from the days when the burgher had to fear the prince and his knights because at any moment he might be spoliated by them. In itself it is no finer,

* [One who has passed his second state examination.—EDITOR.]

nobler, or more honorable to spend one's days in a government office filling out documents than, for example, to work in the blueprint room of a machine factory. The tax collector has no more distinguished an occupation than those who are engaged in creating wealth directly, a part of which is skimmed off in the form of taxes to defray the expenses of the apparatus of government.

This notion of the special distinction and dignity attaching to the exercise of all the functions of government is what constitutes the basis of the pseudodemocratic theory of the state. According to this doctrine, it is shameful for anyone to allow himself to be ruled by others. Its ideal is a constitution in which the whole people rules and governs. This, of course, never has been, never can be, and never will be possible, not even under the conditions prevailing in a small state. It was once thought that this ideal had been realized in the Greek city-states of antiquity and in the small cantons of the Swiss mountains. This too was a mistake. In Greece only a part of the populace, the free citizens, had any share in the government; the metics and slaves had none. In the Swiss cantons only certain matters of a purely local character were and still are settled on the constitutional principle of direct democracy; all affairs transcending these narrow territorial bounds are managed by the Federation, whose government by no means corresponds to the ideal of direct democracy.

It is not at all shameful for a man to allow himself to be ruled by others. Government and administration, the enforcement of police regulations and similar ordinances, also require specialists: professional civil servants and professional politicians. The principle of the division of labor does not stop short even of the functions of government. One cannot be an engineer and a policeman at the same time. It in no way detracts from my dignity, my well-being, or my freedom that I am not myself a policeman. It is no more undemocratic for a few people to have the responsibility of providing protection for everyone else than it is for a few people to undertake to produce shoes for everyone else. There is not the slightest reason to object to professional politicians and professional civil servants if the institutions of the state are democratic. But democracy is something entirely different from what the romantic visionaries who prattle about direct democracy imagine.

Government by a handful of people—and the rulers are always as much in the minority as against those ruled as the producers of shoes are as against the consumers of shoes—depends on the consent of the governed, i.e., on their acceptance of the existing administration. They may see it only as the lesser evil, or as an unavoidable evil, yet they must be of the opinion that a change in the existing situation would have no purpose. But once the majority of the governed becomes convinced that it is necessary and possible to change the form of government and to replace the old regime and the old personnel with a new regime and new personnel, the days of the former are numbered. The majority will have the power to carry out its wishes by force even against the will of the old regime. In the long run no government can maintain itself in power if it does not have public opinion behind it, i.e., if those governed are not convinced that the government is good. The force to which the government resorts in order to make refractory spirits compliant can be successfully applied only as long as the majority does not stand solidly in opposition.

There is, therefore, in every form of polity a means for making the government at least ultimately dependent on the will of the governed, viz., civil war, revolution, insurrection. But it is just this expedient that liberalism wants to avoid. There can be no lasting economic improvement if the peaceful course of affairs is continually interrupted by internal struggles. A political situation such as existed in England at the time of the Wars of the Roses would plunge modern England in a few years into the deepest and most dreadful misery. The present level of economic development would never have been attained if no solution had been found to the problem of preventing the continual outbreak of civil wars. A fratricidal struggle like the French Revolution of 1789 cost a heavy loss in life and property. Our present economy could no longer endure such convulsions. The population of a modern metropolis would have to suffer so frightfully from a revolutionary uprising that could bar the importation of food and coal and cut off the flow of electricity, gas, and water that even the fear that such disturbances might break out would paralyze the life of the city.

Here is where the social function performed by democracy finds its point of application. Democracy is that form of political constitution which makes possible the adaptation of the government to the wishes of the governed without violent struggles. If in a democratic state the government is no longer being conducted as the majority of the population would have it, no civil war is necessary to put into office those who are willing to work to suit the majority. By means of elections and parliamentary arrangements, the change of government is executed smoothly and without friction, violence, or bloodshed.

## 9. Critique of the Doctrine of Force

The champions of democracy in the eighteenth century argued that only monarchs and their ministers are morally depraved, injudicious, and evil. The people, however, are altogether good, pure, and noble, and have, besides, the intellectual gifts needed in order always to know and to do what is right. This is, of course, all nonsense, no less so than the flattery of the courtiers who ascribed all good and noble qualities to their princes. The people are the sum of all individual citizens; and if some individuals are not intelligent and noble, then neither are all together.

Since mankind entered the age of democracy with such high-flown expectations, it is not surprising that disillusionment should soon have set in. It was quickly discovered that the democracies committed at least as many errors as the monarchies and aristocracies had. The comparison that people drew between the men whom the democracies placed at the head of the government and those whom the emperors and kings, in the exercise of their absolute power, had elevated to that position, proved by no means favorable to the new wielders of power. The French are wont to speak of "killing with ridicule." And indeed, the statesmen representative of democracy soon rendered it everywhere ridiculous. Those of the old regime had displayed a certain aristocratic dignity, at least in their outward demeanor. The new ones, who replaced them, made themselves contemptible by their behavior. Nothing has done more harm to democracy in Germany and Austria than the hollow arrogance and impudent vanity with which the Social-Democratic leaders who rose to power after the collapse of the empire conducted themselves.

Thus, wherever democracy triumphed, an antidemocratic doctrine soon arose in fundamental opposition to it. There is no sense, it was said, in allowing the majority to rule. The best ought to govern, even if they are in the minority. This seems so obvious that the supporters of antidemocratic movements of all kinds have steadily increased in number. The more contemptible the men whom democracy has placed at the top have proved themselves to be, the greater has grown the number of the enemies of democracy.

There are, however, serious fallacies in the antidemocratic doctrine. What, after all, does it mean to speak of "the best man" or "the best men"? The Republic of Poland placed a piano virtuoso at its head because it considered him the best Pole of the age. But the qualities that the leader of a state must have are very different from those of a musician. The opponents of democracy, when they use the expression "the best," can mean nothing else than the man or the men best fitted to conduct the affairs of the government, even if they understand little or nothing of music. But this leads to the same political question: Who is the best fitted? Was it Disraeli or Gladstone? The Tory saw the best man in the former; the Whig, in the latter. Who should decide this if not the majority?

And so we reach the decisive point of all antidemocratic doctrines, whether advanced by the descendants of the old aristocracy and the supporters of hereditary monarchy, or by the syndicalists, Bolsheviks, and socialists, viz., the doctrine of force. The opponents of democracy champion the right of a minority to seize control of the state by force and to rule over the majority.

The moral justificátion of this procedure consists, it is thought, precisely in the power actually to seize the reins of government. One recognizes the best, those who alone are competent to govern and command, by virtue of their demonstrated ability to impose their rule on the majority against its will. Here the teaching of *l'Action Française* coincides with that of the syndicalists, and the doctrine of Ludendorff and Hitler, with that of Lenin and Trotzky.

Many arguments can be urged for and against these doctrines, depending on one's religious and philosophical convictions, about which any agreement is scarcely to be expected. This is not the place to present and discuss the arguments pro and con, for they are not conclusive. The only consideration that can be decisive is one that bases itself on the fundamental argument in favor of democracy.

If every group that believes itself capable of imposing its rule on the rest is to be entitled to undertake the attempt, we must be prepared for an uninterrupted series of civil wars. But such a state of affairs is incompatible with the stage of the division of labor that we have reached today. Modern society, based as it is on the division of labor, can be preserved only under conditions of lasting peace. If we had to prepare for the possibility of continual civil wars and internal struggles, we should have to retrogress to such a primitive stage of the division of labor that each province at least, if not each village, would become virtually autarkic, i.e., capable of feeding and maintaining itself for a time as a self-sufficient economic entity without importing anything from the outside. This would mean such an enormous decline in the productivity of labor that the earth could feed only a fraction of the population that it supports today. The antidemocratic ideal leads to the kind of economic order known to the Middle Ages and antiquity. Every city, every village, indeed, every individual dwelling was fortified and equipped for defense, and every province was as independent of the rest of the world as possible in its provision of commodities.

The democrat too is of the opinion that the best man ought

to rule. But he believes that the fitness of a man or of a group of men to govern is better demonstrated if they succeed in convincing their fellow citizens of their qualifications for that position, so that they are voluntarily entrusted with the conduct of public affairs, than if they resort to force to compel others to acknowledge their claims. Whoever does not succeed in attaining to a position of leadership by virtue of the power of his arguments and the confidence that his person inspires has no reason to complain about the fact that his fellow citizens prefer others to him.

To be sure, it should not and need not be denied that there is one situation in which the temptation to deviate from the democratic principles of liberalism becomes very great indeed. If judicious men see their nation, or all the nations of the world, on the road to destruction, and if they find it impossible to induce their fellow citizens to heed their counsel, they may be inclined to think it only fair and just to resort to any means whatever, in so far as it is feasible and will lead to the desired goal, in order to save everyone from disaster. Then the idea of a dictatorship of the elite, of a government by the minority maintained in power by force and ruling in the interests of all, may arise and find supporters. But force is never a means of overcoming these difficulties. The tyranny of a minority can never endure unless it succeeds in convincing the majority of the necessity or, at any rate, of the utility, of its rule. But then the minority no longer needs force to maintain itself in power.

History provides an abundance of striking examples to show that, in the long run, even the most ruthless policy of repression does not suffice to maintain a government in power. To cite but one, the most recent and the best known: when the Bolsheviks seized control in Russia, they were a small minority, and their program found scant support among the great masses of their countrymen. For the peasantry, who constitute the bulk of the Russian people, would have nothing to do with the Bolshevik policy of farm collectivization. What they wanted was the division of the land among the "landed poverty," as the Bolsheviks call this part of the population. And it was this program of the peasantry, not that of the Marxist leaders, which was actually put into effect. In order to remain in power, Lenin and Trotzky not only accepted this agrarian reform, but even made it a part of their own program, which they undertook to defend against all attacks, domestic and foreign. Only thus were the Bolsheviks able to win the confidence of the great mass of the Russian people. Since they adopted this policy of land distribution, the Bolsheviks rule no longer against the will of the great mass of the people, but with their consent and support. There were only two possible alternatives open to them: either their program or their control of the government had to be sacrificed. They chose the first and remained in power. The third possibility, to carry out their program by force against the will of the great mass of the people, did not exist at all. Like every determined and well-led minority, the Bolsheviks were able to seize control by force and retain it for a short time. In the long run, however, they would have been no better able to keep it than any other minority. The various attempts of the Whites to dislodge the Bolsheviks all failed because the mass of the Russian people were against them. But even if they had succeeded, the victors too would have had to respect the desires of the overwhelming majority of the population. It would have been impossible for them to alter in any way after the event the already accomplished fact of the land distribution and to restore to the landowners what had been stolen from them.

Only a group that can count on the consent of the governed can establish a lasting regime. Whoever wants to see the world governed according to his own ideas must strive for dominion over men's minds. It is impossible, in the long run, to subject men against their will to a regime that they reject. Whoever tries to do so by force will ultimately come to grief, and the struggles provoked by his attempt will do more harm than the worst government based on the consent of the governed could ever do. Men cannot be made happy against their will.

## 10. The Argument of Fascism

If liberalism nowhere found complete acceptance, its success in the nineteenth century went so far at least as that some of the most important of its principles were considered beyond dispute. Before 1914, even the most dogged and bitter enemies of liberalism had to resign themselves to allowing many liberal principles to pass unchallenged. Even in Russia, where only a few feeble rays of liberalism had penetrated, the supporters of the Czarist despotism, in persecuting their opponents, still had to take into consideration the liberal opinions of Europe; and during the World War, the war parties in the belligerent nations, with all their zeal, still had to practice a certain moderation in their struggle against internal opposition.

Only when the Marxist Social Democrats had gained the upper hand and taken power in the belief that the age of liberalism and capitalism had passed forever did the last concessions disappear that it had still been thought necessary to make to the liberal ideology. The parties of the Third International consider any means as permissible if it seems to give promise of helping them in their struggle to achieve their ends. Whoever does not unconditionally acknowledge all their teachings as the only correct ones and stand by them through thick and thin has, in their opinion, incurred the penalty of death; and they do not hesitate to exterminate him and his whole family, infants included, whenever and wherever it is physically possible.

The frank espousal of a policy of annihilating opponents and the murders committed in the pursuance of it have given rise to an opposition movement. All at once the scales fell from the eyes of the non-Communist enemies of liberalism. Until then they had believed that even in a struggle against a hateful opponent one still had to respect certain liberal principles. They had had, even though reluctantly, to exclude murder and assassination from the list of measures to be resorted to in political struggles. They had had to resign themselves to many limitations in persecuting the opposition press and in suppressing the spoken word. Now, all at once, they saw that opponents had risen up who gave no heed to such considerations and for whom any means was good enough to defeat an adversary. The militaristic and nationalistic enemies of the Third International felt themselves cheated by liberalism. Liberalism, they thought, stayed their hand when they desired to strike a blow against the revolutionary parties while it was still possible to do so. If liberalism had not hindered them, they would, so they believe, have bloodily nipped the revolutionary movements in the bud. Revolutionary ideas had been able to take root and flourish only because of the tolerance they had been accorded by their opponents, whose will power had been enfeebled by a regard for liberal principles that, as events subsequently proved, was overscrupulous. If the idea had occurred to them years ago that it is permissible to crush ruthlessly every revolutionary movement, the victories that the Third International has won since 1917 would never have been possible. For the militarists and nationalists believe that when it comes to shooting and fighting, they themselves are the most accurate marksmen and the most adroit fighters.

The fundamental idea of these movements—which, from the name of the most grandiose and tightly disciplined among them, the Italian, may, in general, be designated as Fascist—consists in the proposal to make use of the same unscrupulous methods in the struggle against the Third International as the latter employs against its opponents. The Third International seeks to exterminate its adversaries and their ideas in the same way that the hygienist strives to exterminate a pestilential bacillus; it considers itself in no way bound by the terms of any compact that it may conclude with opponents, and it deems any crime, any lie, and any calumny permissible in carrying on its struggle. The Fascists, at least in principle, profess the same intentions. That they have not yet succeeded as fully as the Russian Bolsheviks in freeing themselves from a certain regard for liberal notions and ideas and traditional ethical precepts is to be attributed solely to the fact that the Fascists carry on their work among nations in which the intellectual and moral heritage of some thousands of years of civilization cannot be destroyed at one blow, and not among the barbarian peoples on both sides of the Urals, whose relationship to civilization has never been any other than that of marauding denizens of forest and desert accustomed to engage, from time to time, in predatory raids on civilized lands in the hunt for booty. Because of this difference, Fascism will never succeed as completely as Russian Bolshevism in freeing itself from the power of liberal ideas. Only under the fresh impression of the murders and atrocities perpetrated by the supporters of the Soviets were Germans and Italians able to block out the remembrance of the traditional restraints of justice and morality and find the impulse to bloody counteraction. The deeds of the Fascists and of other parties corresponding to them were emotional reflex actions evoked by indignation at the deeds of the Bolsheviks and Communists. As soon as the first flush of anger had passed, their policy took a more moderate course and will probably become even more so with the passage of time.

This moderation is the result of the fact that traditional liberal views still continue to have an unconscious influence on the Fascists. But however far this may go, one must not fail to recognize that the conversion of the Rightist parties to the tactics of Fascism shows that the battle against liberalism has resulted in successes that, only a short time ago, would have been considered completely unthinkable. Many people approve of the methods of Fascism, even though its economic program is altogether antiliberal and its policy completely interventionist, because it is far from practicing the senseless and unrestrained destructionism that has stamped the Communists as the archenemies of civilization. Still others, in full knowledge of the evil that Fascist economic policy brings with it, view Fascism, in comparison with Bolshevism and Sovietism, as at least the lesser evil. For the majority of its public and secret supporters and admirers, however, its appeal consists precisely in the violence of its methods.

Now it cannot be denied that the only way one can offer effective resistance to violent assaults is by violence. Against the weapons of the Bolsheviks, weapons must be used in reprisal, and it would be a mistake to display weakness before murderers. No liberal has ever called this into question. What distinguishes liberal from Fascist political tactics is not a difference of opinion in regard to the necessity of using armed force to resist armed attackers, but a difference in the fundamental estimation of the role of violence in a struggle for power. The great danger threatening domestic policy from the side of Fascism lies in its complete faith in the decisive power of violence. In order to assure success, one must be imbued with the will to victory and always proceed violently. This is its highest principle. What happens, however, when one's opponent, similarly animated by the will to be victorious, acts just as violently? The result must be a battle, a civil war. The ultimate victor to emerge from such conflicts will be the faction strongest in number. In the long run, a minority—even if it is composed of the most capable and energetic—cannot succeed in resisting the majority. The decisive question, therefore, always remains: How does one obtain a majority for one's own party? This, however, is a purely intellectual matter. It is a victory that can be won only with the weapons of the intellect, never by force. The suppression of all opposition by sheer violence is a most unsuitable way to win adherents to one's cause. Resort to naked force—that is, without justification in terms of intellectual arguments accepted by public opinion— merely gains new friends for those whom one is thereby trying to combat. In a battle between force and an idea, the latter always prevails.

Fascism can triumph today because universal indignation at the infamies committed by the socialists and communists has obtained for it the sympathies of wide circles. But when the fresh impression of the crimes of the Bolsheviks has paled, the socialist program will once again exercise its power of attraction on the masses. For Fascism does nothing to combat it except to suppress socialist ideas and to persecute the people who spread them. If it wanted really to combat socialism, it would have to oppose it with ideas. There is, however, only *one* idea that can be effectively opposed to socialism, viz., that of liberalism.

It has often been said that nothing furthers a cause more than creating martyrs for it. This is only approximately correct. What strengthens the cause of the persecuted faction is not the martyrdom of its adherents, but the fact that they are being attacked by force, and not by intellectual weapons. Repression by brute force is always a confession of the inability to make use of the better weapons of the intellect—better because they alone give promise of final success. This is the fundamental error from which Fascism suffers and which will ultimately cause its downfall. The victory of Fascism in a number of countries is only an episode in the long series of struggles over the problem of property. The next episode will be the victory of Communism. The ultimate outcome of the struggle, however, will not be decided by arms, but by ideas. It is ideas that group men into fighting factions, that press the weapons into their hands, and that determine against whom and for whom the weapons shall be used. It is they alone, and not arms, that, in the last analysis, turn the scales.

So much for the domestic policy of Fascism. That its foreign policy, based as it is on the avowed principle of force in international relations, cannot fail to give rise to an endless series of wars that must destroy all of modern civilization requires no further discussion. To maintain and further raise our present level of economic development, peace among nations must be assured. But they cannot live together in peace if the basic tenet of the ideology by which they are governed is the belief that one's own nation can secure its place in the community of nations by force alone.

It cannot be denied that Fascism and similar movements aiming at the establishment of dictatorships are full of the best intentions and that their intervention has, for the moment, saved European civilization. The merit that Fascism has thereby won for itself will live on eternally in history. But though its policy has brought salvation for the moment, it is not of the kind which could promise continued success. Fascism was an emergency makeshift. To view it as something more would be a fatal error.

## 11. The Limits of Governmental Activity

As the liberal sees it, the task of the state consists solely and exclusively in guaranteeing the protection of life, health, liberty, and private property against violent attacks. Everything that goes beyond this is an evil. A government that, instead of fulfilling its task, sought to go so far as actually to infringe on personal security of life and health, freedom, and property would, of course, be altogether bad.

Still, as Jacob Burckhardt says, power is evil in itself, no matter who exercises it. It tends to corrupt those who wield it and leads to abuse. Not only absolute sovereigns and aristocrats, but the masses also, in whose hands democracy entrusts the supreme power of government, are only too easily inclined to excesses.

In the United States, the manufacture and sale of alcoholic beverages are prohibited. Other countries do not go so far, but nearly everywhere some restrictions are imposed on the sale of opium, cocaine, and similar narcotics. It is universally deemed one of the tasks of legislation and government to protect the individual from himself. Even those who otherwise generally have misgivings about extending the area of governmental activity consider it quite proper that the freedom of the individual should be curtailed in this respect, and they think that only a benighted doctrinairism could oppose such prohibitions. Indeed, so general is the acceptance of this kind of interference by the authorities in the life of the individual that those who are opposed to liberalism on principle are prone to base their argument on the ostensibly undisputed acknowledgment of the necessity of such prohibitions and to draw from it the conclusion that complete freedom is an evil and that some measure of restriction must be imposed upon the freedom of the individual by the governmental authorities in their capacity as guardians of his welfare. The question cannot be whether the authorities ought to impose restrictions upon the freedom of the individual, but only how far they ought to go in this respect.

No words need be wasted over the fact that all these narcotics are harmful. The question whether even a small quantity of alcohol is harmful or whether the harm results only from the abuse of alcoholic beverages is not at issue here. It is an established fact that alcoholism, cocainism, and morphinism are deadly enemies of life, of health, and of the capacity for work and enjoyment; and a utilitarian must therefore consider them as vices. But this is far from demonstrating that the authorities must interpose to suppress these vices by commercial prohibitions, nor is it by any means evident that such intervention on the part of the government is really capable of suppressing them or that, even if this end could be attained, it might not therewith open up a Pandora's box of other dangers, no less mischievous than alcoholism and morphinism.

Whoever is convinced that indulgence or excessive indulgence in these poisons is pernicious is not hindered from living abstemiously or temperately. This question cannot be treated exclusively in reference to alcoholism, morphinism, cocainism, etc., which all reasonable men acknowledge to be evils. For if the majority of citizens is, in principle, conceded the right to impose its way of life upon a minority, it is impossible to stop at prohibitions against indulgence in alcohol, morphine, cocaine, and similar poisons. Why should not what is valid for these poisons be valid also for nicotine, caffein, and the like? Why should not the state generally prescribe which foods may be indulged in and which must be avoided because they are injurious? In sports too, many people are prone to carry their indulgence further than their strength will allow. Why should not the state interfere here as well? Few men know how to be temperate in their sexual life, and it seems especially difficult for aging persons to understand that they should cease entirely to indulge in such pleasures or, at least, do so in moderation. Should not the state intervene here too? More harmful still than all these pleasures, many will say, is the reading of evil literature. Should a press pandering to the lowest instincts of man be allowed to corrupt the soul? Should not the exhibition of pornographic pictures, of obscene plays, in short, of all allurements to immorality, be prohibited? And is not the dissemination of false sociological doctrines just as injurious to men and nations? Should men be permitted to incite others to civil war and to wars against foreign countries? And should scurrilous lampoons and blasphemous diatribes be allowed to undermine respect for God and the Church?

We see that as soon as we surrender the principle that the state should not interfere in any questions touching on the individual's mode of life, we end by regulating and restricting the latter down to the smallest detail. The personal freedom of the individual is abrogated. He becomes a slave of the community, bound to obey the dictates of the majority. It is hardly necessary to expatiate on the ways in which such powers could be abused by malevolent persons in authority. The wielding of powers of this kind even by men imbued with the best of intentions must needs reduce the world to a graveyard of the spirit. All mankind's progress has been achieved as a result of the initiative of a small minority that began to deviate from the ideas and customs of the majority until their example finally moved the others to accept the innovation themselves. To give the majority the right to dictate to the minority what it is to think, to read, and to do is to put a stop to progress once and for all.

Let no one object that the struggle against morphinism and the struggle against "evil" literature are two quite different things. The only difference between them is that some of the same people who favor the prohibition of the former will not agree to the prohibition of the latter. In the United States, the Methodists and Fundamentalists, right after the passage of the law prohibiting the manufacture and sale of alcoholic beverages, took up the struggle for the suppression of the theory of evolution, and they have already succeeded in ousting Darwinism from the schools in a number of states. In Soviet Russia, every free expression of opinion is suppressed. Whether or not permission is granted for a book to be published depends on the discretion of a number of uneducated and uncultivated fanatics who have been placed in charge of the arm of the government empowered to concern itself with such matters.

The propensity of our contemporaries to demand authoritarian prohibition as soon as something does not please them, and their readiness to submit to such prohibitions even when what is prohibited is quite agreeable to them shows how deeply ingrained the spirit of servility still remains within them. It will require many long years of self-education until the subject can turn himself into the citizen. A free man must be able to endure it when his fellow men act and live otherwise than he considers proper. He must free himself from the habit, just as soon as something does not please him, of calling for the police.

## 12. *Tolerance*

Liberalism limits its concern entirely and exclusively to earthly life and earthly endeavor. The kingdom of religion, on the other hand, is not of this world. Thus, liberalism and religion could both exist side by side without their spheres' touching. That they should have reached the point of collision was not the fault of liberalism. It did not transgress its proper sphere; it did not intrude into the domain of religious faith or of metaphysical doctrine. Nevertheless, it encountered the church as a political power claiming the right to regulate according to its judgment not only the relationship of man to the world to come, but also the affairs of this world. It was at this point that the battle lines had to be drawn.

So overwhelming was the victory won by liberalism in this conflict that the church had to give up, once and for all, claims that it had vigorously maintained for thousands of years. The burning of heretics, inquisitorial persecutions, religious wars— these today belong to history. No one can understand any longer how quiet people, who practiced their devotions as they believed right within the four walls of their own home, could have been dragged before courts, incarcerated, martyred, and burned. But even if no more stakes are kindled *ad majorem Dei gloriam,* a great deal of intolerance still persists.

Liberalism, however, must be intolerant of every kind of intolerance. If one considers the peaceful cooperation of all men as the goal of social evolution, one cannot permit the peace to be disturbed by priests and fanatics. Liberalism proclaims tolerance for every religious faith and every metaphysical belief, not out of indifference for these "higher" things, but from the conviction that the assurance of peace within society must take precedence over everything and everyone. And because it demands toleration of all opinions and all churches and sects, it must recall them all to their proper bounds whenever they venture intolerantly beyond them. In a social order based on peaceful cooperation, there is no room for the claim of the churches to monopolize the instruction and education of the young. Everything that their supporters accord them of their own free will may and must be granted to the churches; nothing may be permitted to them in respect to persons who want to have nothing to do with them.

It is difficult to understand how these principles of liberalism could make enemies among the communicants of the various faiths. If they make it impossible for a church to make converts by force, whether its own or that placed at its disposal by the state, on the other hand they also protect that church against coercive proselytization by other churches and sects. What liberalism takes from the church with one hand it gives back again with the other. Even religious zealots must concede that liberalism takes nothing from faith of what belongs to its proper sphere.

To be sure, the churches and sects that, where they have the upper hand, cannot do enough in their persecution of dissenters, also demand, where they find themselves in the minority, tolerance at least for themselves. However, this demand for tolerance has nothing whatever in common with the liberal demand for tolerance. Liberalism demands tolerance as a matter of principle, not from opportunism. It demands toleration even of obviously nonsensical teachings, absurd forms of heterodoxy, and childishly silly superstitions. It demands toleration for doctrines and opinions that it deems detrimental and ruinous to society and even for movements that it indefatigably combats. For what impels liberalism to demand and accord toleration is not consideration for the content of the doctrine to be tolerated, but the knowledge that only tolerance can create and preserve the condition of social peace without which humanity must relapse into the barbarism and penury of centuries long past.

Against what is stupid, nonsensical, erroneous, and evil, liberalism fights with the weapons of the mind, and not with brute force and repression.

### 13. *The State and Antisocial Conduct*

The state is the apparatus of compulsion and coercion. This holds not only for the "night-watchman" state, but just as much for every other, and most of all for the socialist state. Everything that the state is capable of doing it does by compulsion and the application of force. To suppress conduct dangerous to the existence of the social order is the sum and substance of state activity; to this is added, in a socialist community, control over the means of production.

The sober logic of the Romans expressed this fact symbolically by adopting the axe and the bundle of rods as the emblem of the state. Abstruse mysticism, calling itself philosophy, has done as much as possible in modern times to obscure the truth of the matter. For Schelling, the state is the direct and visible image of absolute life, a phase in the revelation of the Absolute or World Soul. It exists only for its own sake, and its activity is directed exclusively to the maintenance of both the substance and the form of its existence. For Hegel, Absolute Reason reveals itself in the state, and Objective Spirit realizes itself in it. It is ethical mind developed into an organic reality—reality and the ethical idea as the revealed substantial will intelligible to itself. The epigones of idealist philosophy outdid even their masters in their deification of the state. To be sure, one comes no closer to the truth if, in reaction to these and similar doctrines, one calls the state, with Nietzsche, the coldest of all cold monsters. The state is neither cold nor warm, for it is an abstract concept in whose name living men—the organs of the state, the government —act. All state activity is human action, an evil inflicted by men on men. The goal—the preservation of society—justifies the action of the organs of the state, but the evils inflicted are not felt as any less evil by those who suffer under them.

The evil that a man inflicts on his fellow man injures both— not only the one to whom it is done, but also the one who does it. Nothing corrupts a man so much as being an arm of the law and making men suffer. The lot of the subject is anxiety, a spirit of servility and fawning adulation; but the pharisaical self-right-eousness, conceit, and arrogrance of the master are no better.

Liberalism seeks to take the sting out of the relationship of the government official to the citizen. In doing so, of course, it does not follow in the footsteps of those romantics who defend the antisocial behavior of the lawbreaker and condemn not only judges and policemen, but also the social order as such. Liberal-ism neither wishes to nor can deny that the coercive power of the state and the lawful punishment of criminals are institutions that society could never, under any circumstances, do without. How-ever, the liberal believes that the purpose of punishment is solely to rule out, as far as possible, behavior dangerous to society. Punishment should not be vindictive or retaliatory. The criminal has incurred the penalties of the law, but not the hate and sadism of the judge, the policeman, and the ever lynch-thirsty mob.

What is most mischievous about the coercive power that justifies itself in the name of the "state" is that, because it is always of necessity ultimately sustained by the consent of the majority, it directs its attack against germinating innovations. Human society cannot do without the apparatus of the state, but the whole of mankind's progress has had to be achieved against the resistance and opposition of the state and its power of coer-cion. No wonder that all who have had something new to offer humanity have had nothing good to say of the state or its laws! Incorrigible etatist mystics and state-worshippers may hold this against them; liberals will understand their position even if they cannot approve it. Yet every liberal must oppose this under-standable aversion to everything that pertains to jailers and policemen when it is carried to the point of such overweening self-esteem as to proclaim the right of the individual to rebel against the state. Violent resistance against the power of the state is the last resort of the minority in its effort to break loose from the oppression of the majority. The minority that desires to see its ideas triumph must strive by intellectual means to become the majority. The state must be so constituted that the scope of its laws permits the individual a certain amount of latitude within which he can move freely. The citizen must not be so narrowly circumscribed in his activities that, if he thinks differently from those in power, his only choice is either to perish or to destroy the machinery of state.

# 2

# Liberal Economic Policy

## 1. *The Organization of the Economy*

It is possible to distinguish five different conceivable systems of organizing the cooperation of individuals in a society based on the division of labor: the system of private ownership of the means of production, which, in its developed form, we call capitalism; the system of private ownership of the means of production with periodic confiscation of all wealth and its subsequent redistribution; the system of syndicalism; the system of public ownership of the means of production, which is known as socialism or communism; and, finally, the system of interventionism.

The history of private ownership of the means of production coincides with the history of the development of mankind from an animal-like condition to the highest reaches of modern civilization. The opponents of private property have gone to great pains to demonstrate that in the primeval beginnings of human society the institution of private property still did not exist in a complete form because a part of the land under cultivation was subject to periodic redistribution. From this observation, which shows that private property is only a "historical category," they have tried to draw the conclusion that it could once again be quite safely dispensed with. The logical fallacy involved in this reasoning is too flagrant to require any further discussion. That there was social cooperation in remote antiquity even in the absence of a completely realized system of private property cannot

60

provide the slightest proof that one could manage without private property just as well at higher stages of civilization. If history could prove anything at all in regard to this question, it could only be that nowhere and at no time has there ever been a people which has raised itself without private property above a condition of the most oppressive penury and savagery scarcely distinguishable from animal existence.

The earlier opponents of the system of private ownership of the means of production did not attack the institution of private property as such, but only the inequality of income distribution. They recommended the abolition of the inequality of income and wealth by means of a system of periodical redistribution of the total quantity of commodities or, at least, of land, which was at that time virtually the only factor of production taken into consideration. In the technologically backward countries, where primitive agricultural production prevails, this idea of an equal distribution of property still holds sway today. People are accustomed to call it agrarian socialism, though the appellation is not at all apposite since this system has nothing to do with socialism. The Bolshevist revolution in Russia, which had begun as socialist, did not establish socialism in agriculture—i.e., communal ownership of the land—but, instead, agrarian socialism. In large areas of the rest of Eastern Europe, the division of big landed estates among the small farmers, under the name of agrarian reform, is the ideal espoused by influential political parties.

It is unnecessary to enter further into a discussion of this system. That it must result in a reduction in the output of human labor will scarcely be disputed. Only where land is still cultivated in the most primitive way can one fail to recognize the decrease in productivity which follows upon its division and distribution. That it is utterly senseless to break up a dairy farm equipped with all the devices of modern technology will be conceded by everyone. As for the transference of this principle of division and distribution to industry or commercial enterprises, it is altogether unthinkable. A railroad, a rolling mill, or a machine factory cannot be divided up. One could undertake to carry out the periodical redistribution of property only if one first completely broke up the economy based on the division of labor and the unhampered market and returned to an economy of self-sufficient farmsteads existing side by side without engaging in exchange.

The idea of syndicalism represents the attempt to adapt the ideal of the equal distribution of property to the circumstances of modern large-scale industry. Syndicalism seeks to invest ownership of the means of production neither in individuals nor in society, but in the workers employed in each industry or branch of production.[1]

Since the proportion in which the material and the personal factors of production are combined is different in the different branches of production, equality in the distribution of property cannot be attained in this way at all. From the very outset the worker will receive a greater portion of property in some branches of industry than in others. One has only to consider the difficulties that must arise from the necessity, continually present in any economy, of shifting capital and labor from one branch of production to another. Will it be possible to withdraw capital from one branch of industry in order thereby more generously to equip another? Will it be possible to remove workers from one branch of production in order to transfer them to another where the quota of capital per worker is smaller? The impossibility of such transfers renders the syndicalist commonwealth utterly absurd and impracticable as a form of social organization. Yet if we assume that over and above the individual groups there exists a central power that is entitled to carry out such transfers, we are no longer dealing with syndicalism, but with socialism. In reality, syndicalism as a social ideal is so absurd that only muddleheads who have not sufficiently thought the problem through have ventured to advocate it on principle.

Socialism or communism is that organization of society in which property—the power of deploying all the means of production—is vested in society, i.e., in the state, as the social apparatus of compulsion and coercion. For a society to be judged as socialist it is of no consequence whether the social dividend is distributed equally or according to some other principle.

Neither is it of decisive significance whether socialism is brought about by a formal transfer of the ownership of all the means of production to the state, the social apparatus of compulsion and coercion, or whether the private owners retain their property in name and the socialization consists in the fact that all these "owners" are entitled to employ the means of production left in their hands only according to instructions issued by the state. If the government decides what is to be produced and how, and to whom it is to be sold, and at what "price," then private property still exists in name only; in reality, all property is already socialized, for the mainspring of economic activity is no longer profit-seeking on the part of entrepreneurs and capitalists, but the necessity of fulfilling an imposed duty and of obeying commands.

Finally, we still have to speak of interventionism. According to a widespread opinion, there is, midway between socialism and capitalism, a third possibility of social organization: the system of private property regulated, controlled, and guided by isolated authoritarian decrees (acts of intervention).

The system of periodical redistribution of property and the system of syndicalism will not be discussed in what follows. These two systems are not generally at issue. No one who is in any way to be taken seriously advocates either one. We have to concern ourselves only with socialism, interventionism, and capitalism.

## 2. Private Property and Its Critics

Man's life is not a state of unalloyed happiness. The earth is no paradise. Although this is not the fault of social institutions, people are wont to hold them responsible for it. The foundation of any and every civilization, including our own, is private ownership of the means of production. Whoever wishes to criticize modern civilization, therefore, begins with private property. It is blamed for everything that does not please the critic, especially those evils that have their origin in the fact that private property has been hampered and restrained in various respects so that its full social potentialities cannot be realized.

The usual procedure adopted by the critic is to imagine how wonderful everything would be if only he had his own way. In his dreams he eliminates every will opposed to his own by raising himself, or someone whose will coincides exactly with his, to the position of absolute master of the world. Everyone who preaches the right of the stronger considers himself as the stronger. He who espouses the institution of slavery never stops to reflect that he himself could be a slave. He who demands restrictions on the liberty of conscience demands it in regard to others, and not for himself. He who advocates an oligarchic form of government always includes himself in the oligarchy, and he who goes into ecstasies at the thought of enlightened despotism or dictatorship is immodest enough to allot to himself, in his daydreams, the role of the enlightened despot or dictator, or, at least, to expect that he himself will become the despot over the despot or the dictator over the dictator. Just as no one desires to see himself in the position of the weaker, of the oppressed, of the overpowered, of the negatively privileged, of the subject without rights; so, under socialism, no one desires himself otherwise than in the role of the general director or the mentor of the general director. In the dream and wish phantasies of socialism there is no other life that would be worth living.

Anticapitalist literature has created a fixed pattern for these phantasies of the daydreamer in the customary opposition between profitability and productivity. What takes place in the capitalist social order is contrasted in thought with what—corresponding to the desires of the critic—would be accomplished in the ideal socialist society. Everything that deviates from this ideal image is characterized as unproductive. That the greatest profitability for private individuals and the greatest productivity for the community do not always coincide was long considered the most serious reproach against the capitalist system. Only in recent years has the knowledge gained ground that in the majority of these cases a socialist community could proceed no differently from the way individuals in a capitalist community do. But even where the alleged opposition actually does exist, it cannot simply be assumed that a socialist society would necessarily do what is right and that the capitalist social order is always to be condemned if it does anything else. The concept of productivity is altogether subjective; it can never provide the starting-point for an objective criticism.

It is not worth while, therefore, to concern ourselves with the musings of our daydream-dictator. In his dream vision, everyone is willing and obedient, ready to execute his commands immediately and punctiliously. But it is quite another question how things must appear in a real, and not merely visionary, socialist society. The assumption that the equal distribution of the total annual output of the capitalist economy among all members of society would suffice to assure everyone a sufficient livelihood is, as simple statistical calculations show, altogether false. Thus, a socialist society could scarcely achieve a perceptible increase in the standard of living of the masses in this way. If it holds out the prospect of well-being, and even riches, for all, it can do so only on the assumption that labor in a socialist society will be more productive than it is under capitalism and that a socialist system will be able to dispense with a number of superfluous—and consequently unproductive—expenditures.

In connection with this second point, one thinks, for example, of the abolition of all those expenses originating in the costs of marketing merchandise, of competition, and of advertising. It is clear that there is no room in a socialist community for such expenditures. Yet one must not forget that the socialist apparatus of distribution too will involve not inconsiderable costs, perhaps even greater than those of a capitalist economy. But this is not the decisive element in our judgment of the significance of these expenses. The socialist assumes, without question, as a matter of course, that in a socialist system the productivity of labor will be at least the same as in a capitalist society, and he seeks to prove that it will be even greater. But the first assumption is by no means as self-evident as the advocates of socialism seem to think. The quantity of things produced in a capitalist society is not independent of the manner in which production is carried on. What is of decisive significance is that at every single stage of each branch of production the special interest of the persons engaged in it is bound up most intimately with the productivity of the particular share of labor being performed. Every worker must exert himself to the utmost, since his wages are determined by the output of his labor, and every entrepreneur must strive to produce more cheaply—i.e., with less expenditure of capital and labor—than his competitors.

Only because of these incentives has the capitalist economy been able to produce the wealth that is at its command. To take exception to the alleged excessive costs of the capitalist marketing apparatus is to take a myopic view of things indeed. Whoever reproaches capitalism with squandering resources because there are many competing haberdashers and even more tobacconists to be found on bustling business streets fails to see that this sales organization is only the end result of an apparatus of production that warrants the greatest productivity of labor. All advances in production have been achieved only because it is in the nature of this apparatus continually to make advances. Only because all entrepreneurs are in constant competition and are mercilessly weeded out if they do not produce in the most profitable manner are methods of production perpetually being improved and refined. Were this incentive to disappear, there would be no further progress in production and no effort to economize in the application of the traditional methods. Consequently, it is completely absurd to pose the question how much could be saved if the costs of advertising were abolished. One must rather ask how much could be produced if competition among producers were abolished. The answer to this question cannot be in doubt.

Men can consume only if they labor, and then only as much as their labor has produced. Now it is the characteristic feature of the capitalist system that it provides each member of society with this incentive to carry on his work with the greatest efficiency and thus achieves the highest output. In a socialist society, this direct connection between the labor of the individual and the goods and services he might thereby enjoy would be lacking. The incentive to work would not consist in the possibility of enjoying the fruit of one's labor, but in the command of the authorities to work and in one's own feeling of duty. The precise demonstration that this organization of labor is unfeasible will be offered in a later chapter.

What is always criticized in the capitalist system is the fact that the owners of the means of production occupy a preferential position. They can live without working. If one views the social order from an individualistic standpoint, one must see in this a serious shortcoming of capitalism. Why should one man be better off than another? But whoever considers things, not from the standpoint of individual persons, but from that of the whole social order, will find that the owners of property can preserve their agreeable position solely on condition that they perform a service indispensable for society. The capitalist can keep his favored position only by shifting the means of production to the application most important for society. If he does not do this—if he invests his wealth unwisely—he will suffer losses, and if he does not correct his mistake in time, he will soon be ruthlessly ousted from his preferential position. He will cease to be a capitalist, and others who are better qualified for it will take his place. In a capitalist society, the deployment of the means of production is always in the hands of those best fitted for it; and whether they want to or not, they must constantly take care to employ the means of production in such a way that they yield the greatest output.

## 3. Private Property and the Government

All those in positions of political power, all governments, all kings, and all republican authorities have always looked askance at private property. There is an inherent tendency in all governmental power to recognize no restraints on its operation and to extend the sphere of its dominion as much as possible. To control everything, to leave no room for anything to happen of its own accord without the interference of the authorities— this is the goal for which every ruler secretly strives. If only private property did not stand in the way! Private property creates for the individual a sphere in which he is free of the state. It sets limits to the operation of the authoritarian will. It allows other forces to arise side by side with and in opposition to political power. It thus becomes the basis of all those activities that are free from violent interference on the part of the state. It is the soil in which the seeds of freedom are nurtured and in which the autonomy of the individual and ultimately all intellectual and material progress are rooted. In this sense, it has even been called the fundamental prerequisite for the development of the individual. But it is only with many reservations that the latter formulation can be considered acceptable, because the customary opposition between individual and collectivity, between individualistic and collective ideas and aims, or even between individualistic and universalistic science, is an empty shibboleth.

Thus, there has never been a political power that voluntarily desisted from impeding the free development and operation of the institution of private ownership of the means of production. Governments tolerate private property when they are compelled to do so, but they do not acknowledge it voluntarily in recognition of its necessity. Even liberal politicians, on gaining power, have usually relegated their liberal principles more or less to the background. The tendency to impose oppressive restraints on private property, to abuse political power, and to refuse to respect or recognize any free sphere outside or beyond the dominion of the state is too deeply ingrained in the mentality of those who control the governmental apparatus of compulsion and coercion for them ever to be able to resist it voluntarily. A liberal government is a *contradictio in adjecto*. Governments must be forced into adopting liberalism by the power of the unanimous opinion of the people; that they could voluntarily become liberal is not to be expected.

It is easy to understand what would constrain rulers to recognize the property rights of their subjects in a society composed exclusively of farmers all of whom were equally rich. In such a social order, every attempt to abridge the right to property would immediately meet with the resistance of a united front of all subjects against the government and thus bring about the latter's fall. The situation is essentially different, however, in a society in which there is not only agricultural but also industrial

production, and especially where there are big business enterprises involving large-scale investments in industry, mining, and
trade. In such a society, it is quite possible for those in control
of the government to take action against private property. In
fact, politically there is nothing more advantageous for a government than an attack on property rights, for it is always an
easy matter to incite the masses against the owners of land
and capital. From time immemorial, therefore, it has been the
idea of all absolute monarchs, of all despots and tyrants, to ally
themselves with the "people" against the propertied classes. The
Second Empire of Louis Napoleon was not the only regime to be
founded on the principle of Caesarism. The Prussian authoritarian state of the Hohenzollerns also took up the idea, introduced
by Lassalle into German politics during the Prussian constitutional struggle, of winning the masses of workers to the battle
against the liberal bourgeoisie by means of a policy of etatism
and interventionism. This was the basic principle of the "social
monarchy" so highly extolled by Schmoller and his school.

In spite of all persecutions, however, the institution of private
property has survived. Neither the animosity of all governments,
nor the hostile campaign waged against it by writers and
moralists and by churches and religions, nor the resentment of
the masses—itself deeply rooted in instinctive envy—has availed
to abolish it. Every attempt to replace it with some other method
of organizing production and distribution has always of itself
promptly proved unfeasible to the point of absurdity. People
have had to recognize that the institution of private property is
indispensable and to revert to it whether they liked it or not.

But for all that, they have still refused to admit that the reason
for this return to the institution of free private ownership of
the means of production is to be found in the fact that an economic system serving the needs and purposes of man's life in
society is, in principle, impracticable except on this foundation.
People have been unable to make up their minds to rid themselves of an ideology to which they have become attached, namely,
the belief that private property is an evil that cannot, at least
for the time being, be dispensed with as long as men have not

yet sufficiently evolved ethically. While governments—contrary to their intentions, of course, and to the inherent tendency of every organized center of power—have reconciled themselves to the existence of private property, they have still continued to adhere firmly—not only outwardly, but also in their own thinking—to an ideology hostile to property rights. Indeed, they consider opposition to private property to be correct in principle and any deviation from it on their part to be due solely to their own weakness or to consideration for the interests of powerful groups.

## 4. The Impracticability of Socialism

People are wont to consider socialism impracticable because they think that men lack the moral qualities demanded by a socialist society. It is feared that under socialism most men will not exhibit the same zeal in the performance of the duties and tasks assigned to them that they bring to their daily work in a social order based on private ownership of the means of production. In a capitalist society, every individual knows that the fruit of his labor is his own to enjoy, that his income increases or decreases according as the output of his labor is greater or smaller. In a socialist society, every individual will think that less depends on the efficiency of his own labor, since a fixed portion of the total output is due him in any case and the amount of the latter cannot be appreciably diminished by the loss resulting from the laziness of any one man. If, as is to be feared, such a conviction should become general, the productivity of labor in a socialist community would drop considerably.

The objection thus raised against socialism is completely sound, but it does not get to the heart of the matter. Were it possible in a socialist community to ascertain the output of the labor of every individual comrade with the same precision with which this is accomplished for each worker by means of economic calculation in the capitalist system, the practicability of socialism would not be dependent on the good will of every individual. Society would be in a position, at least within certain limits, to determine the share of the total output to be allotted to each worker on the basis of the extent of his contribution to production. What renders socialism impracticable is precisely the fact that calculation of this kind is impossible in a socialist society.

In the capitalist system, the calculation of profitability constitutes a guide that indicates to the individual whether the enterprise he is operating ought, under the given circumstances, to be in operation at all and whether it is being run in the most efficient possible way, i.e., at the least cost in factors of production. If an undertaking proves unprofitable, this means that the raw materials, half-finished goods, and labor that are needed in it are employed by other enterprises for an end that, from the standpoint of the consumers, is more urgent and more important, or for the same end, but in a more economical manner (i.e., with a smaller expenditure of capital and labor). When, for instance, hand weaving came to be unprofitable, this signified that the capital and labor employed in weaving by machine yield a greater output and that it is consequently uneconomical to adhere to a method of production in which the same input of capital and labor yields a smaller output.

If a new enterprise is being planned, one can calculate in advance whether it can be made profitable at all and in what way. If, for example, one has the intention of constructing a railroad line, one can, by estimating the traffic to be expected and its ability to pay the freight rates, calculate whether it pays to invest capital and labor in such an undertaking. If the result of this calculation shows that the projected railroad promises no profit, this is tantamount to saying that there is other, more urgent employment for the capital and the labor that the construction of the railroad would require; the world is not yet rich enough to be able to afford such an expenditure. But it is not only when the question arises whether or not a given undertaking is to be begun at all that the calculation of value and profitability is decisive; it controls every single step that the entrepreneur takes in the conduct of his business.

Capitalist economic calculation, which alone makes rational production possible, is based on monetary calculation. Only because the prices of all goods and services in the market can be expressed in terms of money is it possible for them, in spite of their heterogeneity, to enter into a calculation involving homogeneous units of measurement. In a socialist society, where all the means of production are owned by the community, and where, consequently, there is no market and no exchange of productive goods and services, there can also be no money prices for goods and services of higher order. Such a social system would thus, of necessity, be lacking in the means for the rational management of business enterprises, viz., economic calculation. For economic calculation cannot take place in the absence of a common denominator to which all the heterogeneous goods and services can be reduced.

Let us consider a quite simple case. For the construction of a railroad from A to B several routes are conceivable. Let us suppose that a mountain stands between A and B. The railroad can be made to run over the mountain, around the mountain, or, by way of a tunnel, through the mountain. In a capitalist society, it is a very easy matter to compute which line will prove the most profitable. One ascertains the cost involved in constructing each of the three lines and the differences in operating costs necessarily incurred by the anticipated traffic on each. From these quantities it is not difficult to determine which stretch of road will be the most profitable. A socialist society could not make such calculations. For it would have no possible way of reducing to a uniform standard of measurement all the heterogeneous quantities and qualities of goods and services that here come into consideration. In the face of the ordinary, everyday problems which the management of an economy presents, a socialist society would stand helpless, for it would have no possible way of keeping its accounts.

The prosperity that has made it possible for many more people to inhabit the earth today than in the precapitalist era is due solely to the capitalist method of lengthy chains of production, which necessarily requires monetary calculation. This is impossible under socialism. In vain have socialist writers labored to demonstrate how one could still manage even without monetary and price calculation. All their efforts in this respect have met with failure.

The leadership of a socialist society would thus be confronted by a problem that it could not possibly solve. It would not be able to decide which of the innumerable possible modes of procedure is the most rational. The resulting chaos in the economy would culminate quickly and irresistibly in universal impoverishment and a retrogression to the primitive conditions under which our ancestors once lived.

The socialist ideal, carried to its logical conclusion, would eventuate in a social order in which all the means of production were owned by the people as a whole. Production would be completely in the hands of the government, the center of power in society. It alone would determine what was to be produced and how, and in what way goods ready for consumption were to be distributed. It makes little difference whether we imagine this socialist state of the future as democratically constituted or otherwise. Even a democratic socialist state would necessarily constitute a tightly organized bureaucracy in which everyone, apart from the highest officials, though he might very well, in his capacity as a voter, have participated in some fashion in framing the directives issued by the central authority, would be in the subservient position of an administrator bound to carry them out obediently.

A socialist state of this kind is not comparable to the state enterprises, no matter how vast their scale, that we have seen developing in the last decades in Europe, especially in Germany and Russia. The latter all flourish *side by side with* private ownership of the means of production. They engage in commercial transactions with enterprises that capitalists own and manage, and they receive various stimuli from these enterprises that invigorate their own operation. State railroads, for instance, are provided by their suppliers, the manufacturers of locomotives, coaches, signal installations, and other equipment, with apparatus that has proved successful elsewhere in the operation of privately owned railroads. Thence they receive the incentive to institute innovations in order to keep up with the progress in technology and in methods of business management that is taking place all around them.

It is a matter of common knowledge that national and municipal enterprises have, on the whole, failed, that they are expensive and inefficient, and that they have to be subsidized out of tax funds just to maintain themselves in operation. Of course, where a public enterprise occupies a monopolistic position—as is, for instance, generally the case with municipal transportation facilities and electric light and power plants—the bad consequences of inefficiency need not always express themselves in visible financial failure. Under certain circumstances it may be possible to conceal it by making use of the opportunity open to the monopolist of raising the price of his products and services high enough to render these enterprises, in spite of their uneconomic management, still profitable. The lower productivity of the socialist method of production merely manifests itself differently here and is not so easily recognized as otherwise; essentially, however, the case remains the same.

But none of these experiments in the socialist management of enterprises can afford us any basis for judging what it would mean if the socialist ideal of the communal ownership of *all* means of production were to be realized. In the socialist society of the future, which will leave no room whatsoever for the free activity of private enterprises operating side by side with those owned and controlled by the state, the central planning board will lack entirely the gauge provided for the whole economy by the market and market prices. In the market, where all goods and services come to be traded, exchange ratios, expressed in money prices, may be determined for everything bought and sold. In a social order based on private property, it thus becomes possible to resort to monetary calculation in checking on the results of all economic activities. The social productivity of every economic transaction may be tested by the methods of bookkeeping and cost accounting. It yet remains to be shown that public enterprises are unable to make use of cost accounting in the same way as private enterprises do. Nevertheless, monetary calculation does give even governmental and communal enterprises some basis for judging the success or failure of their management. In a completely socialist economic system, this would be quite impossible, for in the absence of private ownership of the means of production, there could be no exchange of capital goods in the market and consequently neither money prices nor monetary calculation. The general management of a purely socialist society will therefore have no means of reducing to a common denominator the costs of production of all the heterogeneous commodities that it plans to produce.

Nor can this be achieved by setting expenditures in kind against savings in kind. One cannot calculate if it is not possible to reduce to a common medium of expression hours of labor of various grades, iron, coal, building materials of every kind, machines, and all the other things needed in the operation and management of different enterprises. Calculation is possible only when one is able to reduce to monetary terms all the goods under consideration. Of course, monetary calculation has its imperfections and deficiencies, but we have nothing better to put in its place. It suffices for the practical purposes of life as long as the monetary system is sound. If we were to renounce monetary calculation, every economic computation would become absolutely impossible.

This is the decisive objection that economics raises against the possibility of a socialist society. It must forgo the intellectual division of labor that consists in the cooperation of all entrepreneurs, landowners, and workers as producers and consumers in the formation of market prices. But without it, rationality, i.e., the possibility of economic calculation, is unthinkable.

## 5. Interventionism

The socialist ideal is now beginning to lose more and more of its adherents. The penetrating economic and sociological investigations of the problems of socialism that have shown it to be impracticable have not remained without effect, and the failures in which socialist experiments everywhere have ended have disconcerted even its most enthusiastic supporters. Gradually people are once more beginning to realize that society cannot do without private property. Yet the hostile criticism to which the system of private ownership of the means of production has been subjected for decades has left behind such a strong prejudice against the capitalist system that, in spite of their knowledge of the inadequacy and impracticability of socialism, people cannot make up their minds to admit openly that they must return to liberal views on the question of property. To be sure, it is conceded that socialism, the communal ownership of the means of production, is altogether, or at least for the present, impracticable. But, on the other hand, it is asserted that unhampered private ownership of the means of production is also an evil. Thus people want to create a third way, a form of society standing midway between private ownership of the means of production, on the one hand, and communal ownership of the means of production, on the other. Private property will be permitted to exist, but the ways in which the means of production are employed by the entrepreneurs, capitalists, and landowners will be regulated, guided, and controlled by authoritarian decrees and prohibitions. In this way, one forms the conceptual image of a regulated market, of a capitalism circumscribed by authoritarian rules, of private property shorn of its allegedly harmful concomitant features by the intervention of the authorities.

One can best acquire an insight into the meaning and nature of this system by considering a few examples of the consequences of government interference. The crucial acts of intervention with which we have to deal aim at fixing the prices of goods and services at a height different from what the unhampered market would have determined.

In the case of prices formed on the unhampered market, or which would have been formed in the absence of interference on the part of the authorities, the costs of production are covered by the proceeds. If a lower price is decreed by the government, the proceeds will fall short of the costs. Merchants and manufacturers will, therefore, unless the storage of the goods involved would cause them to deteriorate rapidly in value, withhold their merchandise from the market in the hope of more favorable times, perhaps in the expectation that the government order will soon be rescinded. If the authorities do not want the goods concerned to disappear altogether from the market as a result of their interference, they cannot limit themselves to fixing the price; they must at the same time also decree that all stocks on hand be sold at the prescribed price.

But even this does not suffice. At the price determined on the unhampered market, supply and demand would have coincided. Now, because the price was fixed lower by government decree, the demand has increased while the supply has remained unchanged. The stocks on hand are not sufficient to satisfy fully all who are prepared to pay the prescribed price. A part of the demand will remain unsatisfied. The mechanism of the market, which otherwise tends to equalize supply and demand by means of price fluctuations, no longer operates. Now people who would have been prepared to pay the price prescribed by the authorities must leave the market with empty hands. Those who were on line earlier or who were in a position to exploit some personal connection with the sellers have already acquired the whole stock; the others have to go unprovided. If the government wishes to avoid this consequence of its intervention, which runs counter to its intentions, it must add rationing to price control and compulsory sale: a governmental regulation must determine how much of a commodity may be supplied to each individual applicant at the prescribed price.

But once the supplies already on hand at the moment of the government's intervention are exhausted, an incomparably more difficult problem arises. Since production is no longer profitable if the goods are to be sold at the price fixed by the government, it will be reduced or entirely suspended. If the government wishes to have production continue, it must compel the manufacturers to produce, and, to this end, it must also fix the prices of raw materials and half-finished goods and the wages of labor. Its decrees to this effect, however, cannot be limited to only the one or the few branches of production that the authorities wish to regulate because they deem their products especially important.

They must encompass all branches of production. They must regulate the price of all commodities and all wages. In short, they must extend their control over the conduct of all entrepreneurs, capitalists, landowners, and workers. If some branches of production are left free, capital and labor will flow into these, and the government will fail to attain the goal that it wished to achieve by its first act of intervention. But the object of the authorities is that there should be an abundance of production in precisely that branch of industry which, because of the importance they attach to its products, they have especially singled out for regulation. It runs altogether counter to their design that precisely in consequence of their intervention this branch of production should be neglected.

It is therefore clearly evident that an attempt on the part of the government to interfere with the operation of the economic system based on private ownership of the means of production fails of the goal that its authors wished to achieve by means of it. It is, from the point of view of its authors, not only futile, but downright contrary to purpose, because it enormously augments the very "evil" that it was supposed to combat. Before the price controls were decreed, the commodity was, in the opinion of the government, too expensive; now it disappears from the market altogether. This, however, is not the result aimed at by the government, which wanted to make the commodity accessible to the consumer at a cheaper price. On the contrary: from its viewpoint, the absence of the commodity, the impossibility of securing it, must appear as by far the greater evil. In this sense one can say of the intervention of the authorities that it is futile and contrary to the purpose that it was intended to serve, and of the system of economic policy that attempts to operate by means of such acts of intervention that it is impracticable and unthinkable, that it contradicts economic logic.

If the government will not set things right again by desisting from its interference, i.e., by rescinding the price controls, then it must follow up the first step with others. To the prohibition against asking any price higher than the prescribed one it must add not only measures to compel the sale of all stocks on hand under a system of enforced rationing, but price ceilings on goods of higher order, wage controls, and, ultimately, compulsory labor for entrepreneurs and workers. And these regulations cannot be limited to one or a few branches of production, but must encompass them all. There is simply no other choice than this: either to abstain from interference in the free play of the market, or to delegate the entire management of production and distribution to the government. Either capitalism or socialism: there exists no middle way.

The mechanism of the series of events just described is well known to all who have witnessed the attempts of governments in time of war and during periods of inflation to fix prices by fiat. Everyone knows nowadays that government price controls had no other result than the disappearance from the market of the goods concerned. Wherever the government resorts to the fixing of prices, the result is always the same. When, for instance, the government fixes a ceiling on residential rents, a housing shortage immediately ensues. In Austria, the Social Democratic Party has virtually abolished residential rent. The consequence is that in the city of Vienna, for example, in spite of the fact that the population has declined considerably since the beginning of the World War and that several thousand new houses have been constructed by the municipality in the meantime, many thousands of persons are unable to find accommodations.

Let us take still another example: the fixing of minimum wage rates.

When the relationship between employer and employee is left undisturbed by legislative enactments or by violent measures on the part of trade unions, the wages paid by the employer for every type of labor are exactly as high as the increment of value that it adds to the materials in production. Wages cannot rise any higher than this because, if they did, the employer could no longer make a profit and hence would be compelled to discontinue a line of production that did not pay. But neither can wages fall any lower, because then the workers would turn to other branches of industry where they would be better rewarded, so that the employer would be forced to discontinue production because of a labor shortage.

There is, therefore, in the economy always a wage rate at which all workers find employment and every entrepreneur who wishes to undertake some enterprise still profitable at that wage finds workers. This wage rate is customarily called by economists the "static" or "natural" wage. It increases if, other things being equal, the number of workers diminishes; it decreases if, other things being equal, the available quantity of capital for which employment in production is sought suffers any diminution. However, one must, at the same time, observe that it is not quite precise to speak simply of "wages" and "labor." Labor services vary greatly in quality and quantity (calculated per unit of time), and so too do the wages of labor.

If the economy never varied from the stationary state, then in a labor market unhampered by interference on the part of the government or by coercion on the part of the labor unions there would be no unemployed. But the stationary state of society is merely an imaginary construction of economic theory, an intellectual expedient indispensable for our thinking, that enables us, by contrast, to form a clear conception of the processes actually taking place in the economy which surrounds us and in which we live. Life—fortunately, we hasten to add—is never at rest. There is never a standstill in the economy, but perpetual changes, movement, innovation, the continual emergence of the unprecedented. There are, accordingly, always branches of production that are being shut down or curtailed because the demand for their products has fallen off, and other branches of production that are being expanded or even embarked upon for the first time. If we think only of the last few decades, we can at once enumerate a great number of new industries that have sprung up: e.g., the automobile industry, the airplane industry, the motion picture industry, the rayon industry, the canned goods industry, and the radio broadcasting industry. These branches of industry today employ millions of workers, only some of whom have been drawn from the increase in population. Some came from branches of production that were shut down, and even more from those that, as a result of technological improvements, are now able to manage with fewer workers.

Occasionally the changes that occur in the relations among individual branches of production take place so slowly that no worker is obliged to shift to a new type of job; only young people, just beginning to earn their livelihood, will enter, in greater proportion, the new or expanding industries, Generally, however, in the capitalist system, with its rapid strides in improving human welfare, progress takes place too swiftly to spare individuals the necessity of adapting themselves to it. When, two hundred years or more ago, a young lad learned a craft, he could count on practicing it his whole life long in the way he had learned it, without any fear of being injured by his conservatism. Things are different today. The worker too must adjust himself to changing conditions, must add to what he has learned, or begin learning anew. He must leave occupations which no longer require the same number of workers as previously and enter one which has just come into being or which now needs more workers than before. But even if he remains in his old job, he must learn new techniques when circumstances demand it.

All this affects the worker in the form of changes in wage rates. If a particular branch of business employs relatively too many workers, it discharges some, and those discharged will not easily find new work in the same branch of business. The pressure on the labor market exercised by the discharged workers depresses wages in this branch of production. This, in turn, induces the worker to look for employment in those branches of production that wish to attract new workers and are therefore prepared to pay higher wages.

From this it becomes quite clear what must be done in order to satisfy the workers' desire for employment and for high wages. Wages in general cannot be pushed above the height that they would normally occupy in a market unhampered either by government interference or other institutional pressures without creating certain side effects that cannot be desirable for the worker. Wages can be driven up in an individual industry or an individual country if the transfer of workers from other industries or their immigration from other countries is prohibited. Such wage increases are effected at the expense of the workers whose entrance is barred. Their wages are now lower than they would have been if their freedom of movement had not been hindered. The rise in wages of one group is thus achieved at the expense of the others. This policy of obstructing the free movement of labor can benefit only the workers in countries and industries suffering from a relative labor shortage. In an industry or a country where this is not the case, there is only *one* thing that can raise wages: a rise in the general productivity of labor, whether by virtue of an increase in the capital available or through an improvement in the technological processes of production.

If, however, the government fixes minimum wages by law above the height of the static or natural wage, then the employers will find that they are no longer in a position to carry on successfully a number of enterprises that were still profitable when wages stood at the lower point. They will consequently curtail production and discharge workers. The effect of an artificial rise in wages, i.e., one imposed upon the market from the outside, is, therefore, the spread of unemployment.

Now, of course, no attempt is being made today to fix minimum wage rates by law on a large scale. But the position of power that the trade unions occupy has enabled them to do so even in the absence of any positive legislation to that effect. The fact that workers form unions for the purpose of bargaining with the employers does not, in and of itself, necessarily provoke disturbances in the operation of the market. Even the fact that they successfully arrogate to themselves the right to break, without notice, contracts duly entered into by them and to lay down their tools would not itself result in any further disturbance in the labor market. What does create a new situation in the labor market is the element of coercion involved in strikes and compulsory union membership that prevails today in most of the industrial countries of Europe. Since the unionized workers deny access to employment to those who are not members of their union, and resort to open violence during strikes to prevent other workers from taking the place of those on strike, the wage demands that the unions present to the employers have precisely the same force as government decrees fixing minimum wage rates. For the employer must, if he does not wish to shut down his whole enterprise, yield to the demands of the union. He must pay wages such that the volume of production has to be restricted, because what costs more to produce cannot find as large a market as what costs less. Thus, the higher wages exacted by the trade unions become a cause of unemployment.

The unemployment originating from this source differs entirely in extent and duration from that which arises from the changes constantly taking place in the kind and quality of the labor demanded in the market. If unemployment had its cause only in the fact that there is constant progress in industrial development, it could neither assume great proportions nor take on the character of a lasting institution. The workers who can no longer be employed in one branch of production soon find accommodation in others which are expanding or just coming into being. When workers enjoy freedom of movement and the shift from one industry to another is not impeded by legal and other obstacles of a similar kind, adjustment to new conditions takes place without too much difficulty and rather quickly. For the rest, the setting up of labor exchanges would contribute much toward reducing still further the extent of this type of unemployment.

But the unemployment produced by the interference of coercive agencies in the operation of the labor market is no transitory phenomenon continually appearing and disappearing. It is incurable as long as the cause that called it into existence continues to operate, i.e., as long as the law or the violence of the trade unions prevents wages from being reduced, by the pressure of the jobless seeking employment, to the level that they would have reached in the absence of interference on the part of the government or the unions, namely, the rate at which all those eager for work ultimately find it.

For the unemployed to be granted support by the government or by the unions only serves to enlarge the evil. If what is involved is a case of unemployment springing from dynamic changes in the economy, then the unemployment benefits only result in postponing the adjustment of the workers to the new conditions. The jobless worker who is on relief does not consider it necessary to look about for a new occupation if he no longer finds a position in his old one; at least, he allows more time to elapse before he decides to shift to a new occupation or to a new locality or before he reduces the wage rate he demands to that at which he could find work. If unemployment benefits are not set too low, one can say that as long as they are offered, unemployment cannot disappear.

If, however, the unemployment is produced by the artificial raising of the height of wage rates in consequence of the direct intervention of the government or of its toleration of coercive practices on the part of the trade unions, then the only question is who is to bear the costs involved, the employers or the workers. The state, the government, the community never do so; they load them either onto the employer or onto the worker or partially onto each. If the burden falls on the workers, then they are deprived entirely or partially of the fruits of the artificial wage increase they have received; they may even be made to bear more of these costs than the artificial wage increase yielded them. The employer can be saddled with the burden of unemployment benefits to some extent by having to pay a tax proportionate to the total amount of wages paid out by him. In this case, unemployment insurance, by raising the costs of labor, has the same effect as a further increase in wages above the static level: the profitability of the employment of labor is reduced, and the number of workers who still can be profitably engaged is concomitantly decreased. Thus, unemployment spreads even further, in an ever widening spiral. The employers can also be drawn on to pay the costs of the unemployment benefits by means of a tax on their profits or capital, without regard for the number of workers employed. But this too only tends to spread unemployment even further. For when capital is consumed or when the formation of new capital is at least slowed down, the conditions for the employment of labor become, *ceteris paribus,* less favorable.[2]

It is obviously futile to attempt to eliminate unemployment by embarking upon a program of public works that would otherwise not have been undertaken. The necessary resources for such projects must be withdrawn by taxes or loans from the application they would otherwise have found. Unemployment in one industry can, in this way, be mitigated only to the extent that it is increased in another.

From whichever side we consider interventionism, it becomes evident that this system leads to a result that its originators and advocates did not intend and that, even from their standpoint, it must appear as a senseless, self-defeating, absurd policy.

### 6. Capitalism: The Only Possible System of Social Organization

Every examination of the different conceivable possibilities of organizing society on the basis of the division of labor must always come to the same result: there is only the choice between communal ownership and private ownership of the means of production. All intermediate forms of social organization are unavailing and, in practice, must prove self-defeating. If one further realizes that socialism too is unworkable, then one cannot avoid acknowledging that capitalism is the only feasible system of social organization based on the division of labor. This result of theoretical investigation will not come as a surprise to the historian or the philosopher of history. If capitalism has succeeded in maintaining itself in spite of the enmity it has always encountered from both governments and the masses, if it has not been obliged to make way for other forms of social cooperation that have enjoyed to a much greater extent the sympathies of theoreticians and of practical men of affairs, this is to be attributed only to the fact that no other system of social organization is feasible.

Nor is there any further need to explain why it is impossible for us to return to the forms of social and economic organization characteristic of the Middle Ages. Over the whole area now inhabited by the modern nations of Europe the medieval economic system was able to support only a fraction of the number of people who now dwell in that region, and it placed much less in the way of material goods at the disposal of each individual for the provision of his needs than the capitalist form of production supplies men with today. A return to the Middle Ages is out of the question if one is not prepared to reduce the population to a tenth or a twentieth part of its present number and, even further, to oblige every individual to be satisfied with a modicum so small as to be beyond the imagination of modern man.

All the writers who represent the return to the Middle Ages, or, as they put it, to the "new" Middle Ages, as the only social ideal worth striving for reproach the capitalist era above all for its materialistic attitude and mentality. Yet they themselves are much more deeply committed to materialistic views than they believe. For it is nothing but the crassest materialism to think, as many of these writers do, that after reverting to the forms of political and economic organization characteristic of the Middle Ages, society could still retain all the technological improvements in production created by capitalism and thus preserve the high degree of productivity of human labor that it has attained in the capitalist era. The productivity of the capitalist mode of production is the outcome of the capitalist mentality and of the capitalist approach to man and to the satisfaction of man's wants; it is a result of modern technology only in so far as the development of technology must, of necessity, follow from the capitalist mentality. There is scarcely anything so absurd as the fundamental principle of Marx's materialist interpretation of history: "The hand mill made feudal society; the steam mill, capitalist society." It was precisely capitalist society that was needed to create the necessary conditions for the original conception of the steam mill to be developed and put into effect. It was capitalism that created the technology, and not the other way round. But no less absurd is the notion that the technological and material appurtenances of our economy could be preserved even if the intellectual foundations on which they are based were destroyed. Economic activity can no longer be carried on rationally once the prevailing mentality has reverted to traditionalism and faith in authority. The entrepreneur, the catalytic agent, as it were, of the capitalist economy and, concomitantly, also of modern technology, is inconceivable in an environment in which everyone is intent solely on the contemplative life.

If one characterizes as unfeasible every system other than that based on private ownership of the means of production, it follows necessarily that private property must be maintained as the basis of social cooperation and association and that every attempt to abolish it must be vigorously combatted. It is for this reason that liberalism defends the institution of private property against every attempt to destroy it. When, therefore, people call the liberals apologists for private property, they are completely justified, for the Greek word from which "apologist" is derived means the same as "defender." Of course, it would be better to avoid using the foreign word and to be content to express oneself in plain English. For to many people the expressions "apology" and "apologist" convey the connotation that what is being defended is unjust.

Much more important, however, than the rejection of any pejorative suggestion that may be involved in the use of these expressions is the observation that the institution of private property requires no defense, justification, support, or explanation. The continued existence of society depends upon private property, and since men have need of society, they must hold fast to the institution of private property to avoid injuring their own interests as well as the interests of everyone else. For society can continue to exist only on the foundation of private property. Whoever champions the latter champions by the same token the preservation of the social bond that unites mankind, the preservation of culture and civilization. He is an apologist and defender of society, culture, and civilization, and because he desires them as ends, he must also desire and defend the one means that leads to them, namely, private property.

To advocate private ownership of the means of production is by no means to maintain that the capitalist social system, based on private property, is perfect. There is no such thing as earthly perfection. Even in the capitalist system something or other, many things, or even everything, may not be exactly to the liking of this or that individual. But it is the only possible social system. One may undertake to modify one or another of its features as long as in doing so one does not affect the essence and foundation of the whole social order, viz., private property. But by and large we must reconcile ourselves to this system because there simply cannot be any other.

In Nature too, much may exist that we do not like. But we cannot change the essential character of natural events. If, for example, someone thinks—and there are some who have maintained as much—that the way in which man ingests his food, digests it, and incorporates it into his body is disgusting, one cannot argue the point with him. One must say to him: There is only this way or starvation. There is no third way. The same is true of property: either-or—either private ownership of the means of production, or hunger and misery for everyone.

The opponents of liberalism are wont to call its economic doctrine "optimistic." They intend this epithet either as a reproach or as a derisive characterization of the liberal way of thinking.

If by calling the liberal doctrine "optimistic" one means that liberalism considers the capitalist world as the best of all worlds, then this is nothing but pure nonsense. For an ideology based, like that of liberalism, entirely on scientific grounds, such questions as whether the capitalist system is good or bad, whether or not a better one is conceivable, and whether it ought to be rejected on certain philosophic or metaphysical grounds are entirely irrelevant. Liberalism is derived from the pure sciences of economics and sociology, which make no value judgments within their own spheres and say nothing about what ought to be or about what is good and what is bad, but, on the contrary, only ascertain what is and how it comes to be. When these sciences show us that of all the conceivable alternative ways of organizing society only one, viz., the system based on private ownership of the means of production, is capable of being realized, because all other conceivable systems of social organization are unworkable, there is absolutely nothing in this that can justify the designation "optimistic." That capitalism is practicable and workable is a conclusion that has nothing to do with optimism.

To be sure, the opponents of liberalism are of the opinion that this society is very bad. As far as this assertion contains a value judgment, it is naturally not open to any discussion that intends to go beyond highly subjective and therefore unscientific opinions. As far, however, as it is founded on an incorrect understanding of what takes place within the capitalist system, economics and sociology can rectify it. This too is not optimism. Entirely aside from everything else, even the discovery of a great many deficiencies in the capitalist system would not have the slightest significance for the problems of social policy as long as it has not been shown, not that a different social system would be better, but that it would be capable of being realized at all. But this has not been done. Science has succeeded in showing that every system of social organization that could be conceived as a substitute for the capitalist system is self-contradictory and unavailing, so that it could not bring about the results aimed at by its proponents.

How little one is justified in speaking in this connection of "optimism" and "pessimism" and how much the characterization of liberalism as "optimistic" aims at surrounding it with an unfavorable aura by bringing in extrascientific, emotional considerations is best shown by the fact that one can, with as much justice, call those people "optimists" who are convinced that the construction of a socialist or of an interventionist commonwealth would be practicable.

Most of the writers who concern themselves with economic questions never miss an opportunity to heap senseless and childish abuse on the capitalist system and to praise in enthusiastic terms either socialism or interventionism, or even agrarian socialism and syndicalism, as excellent institutions. On the other hand, there have been a few writers who, even if in much milder terms, have sung the praises of the capitalist system. One may, if one wishes, call these writers "optimists." But if one does so, then one would be a thousand times more justified in calling the antiliberal writers "hyperoptimists" of socialism, interventionism, agrarian socialism, and syndicalism. The fact that this does not happen, but that, instead, only liberal writers like Bastiat are called "optimists," shows clearly that in these cases what we are dealing with is not an attempt at a truly scientific classification, but nothing more than a partisan caricature.

What liberalism maintains is, we repeat, by no means that capitalism is good when considered from some particular point of view. What it says is simply that for the attainment of the ends that men have in mind only the capitalist system is suitable and that every attempt to realize a socialist, interventionist, agrarian socialist, or syndicalist society must necessarily prove unsuccessful. Neurotics who could not bear this truth have called economics a dismal science. But economics and sociology are no more dismal because they show us the world as it really is than the other sciences are—mechanics, for instance, because it teaches the impracticability of perpetual motion, or biology because it teaches us the mortality of all living things.

## 7. Cartels, Monopolies, and Liberalism

The opponents of liberalism assert that the necessary preconditions for the adoption of the liberal program no longer exist in the contemporary world. Liberalism was still practicable when many concerns of medium size were engaged in keen competition in each industry. Nowadays, since trusts, cartels, and other monopolistic enterprises are in complete control of the market, liberalism is as good as done for in any case. It is not politics that has destroyed it, but a tendency inherent in the inexorable evolution of the system of free enterprise.

The division of labor gives a specialized function to each productive unit in the economy. This process never stops as long as economic development continues. We long ago passed the stage at which the same factory produced all types of machines. Today a machine factory that does not limit itself exclusively to the production of certain types of machinery is no longer able to meet competition. With the progress of specialization, the area served by an individual supplier must continue to widen. The market supplied by a textile mill that produces only a few kinds of fabrics must be larger than that served by a weaver who weaves every kind of cloth. Undoubtedly this progressive specialization of production tends toward the development in every field of enterprises that have the whole world for their market. If this development is not opposed by protectionist and other anticapitalist measures, the result will be that in every branch of production there will be a relatively small number of concerns, or even only a single concern, intent on producing with the highest degree of specialization and on supplying the whole world.

Today, of course, we are very far from this state of affairs, since the policy of all governments aims at snipping off from the unity of the world economy small areas in which, under the protection of tariffs and other measures designed to achieve the same result, enterprises that would no longer be able to meet competition on the free world market are artificially preserved or even first called into being. Apart from considerations of commercial policy, measures of this kind, which are directed against the concentration of business, are defended on the ground that they alone have prevented the consumers from being exploited by monopolistic combinations of producers.

In order to assess the validity of this argument, we shall assume that the division of labor throughout the whole world has already advanced so far that the production of every article offered for sale is concentrated in a single concern, so that the consumer, in his capacity as a buyer, is always confronted with only a single seller. Under such conditions, according to an ill-considered economic doctrine, the producers would be in a position to keep prices pegged as high as they wished, to realize exorbitant profits, and thereby to worsen considerably the standard of living of the consumers. It is not difficult to see that this idea is completely mistaken. Monopoly prices, if they are not made possible by certain acts of intervention on the part of the government, can be lastingly exacted only on the basis of control over mineral and other natural resources. An isolated monopoly in manufacturing that yielded greater profits than those yielded elsewhere would stimulate the formation of rival firms whose competition would break the monopoly and restore prices and profits to the general rate. Monopolies in manufacturing industries cannot, however, become general, since at every given level of wealth in an economy the total quantity of capital invested and of available labor employed in production—and consequently also the amount of the social product—is a given magnitude. In any particular branch of production, or in several, the amount of capital and labor employed could be reduced in order to increase the price per unit and the aggregate profit of the monopolist or monopolists by curtailing production. The capital and labor thereby freed would then flow into another industry. If, however, all industries attempt to curtail production in order to realize higher prices, they forthwith free labor and capital which, because they are offered at lower rates, will provide a strong stimulus to the formation of new enterprises that must again destroy the monopolistic position of the others. The idea of a universal cartel and monopoly of the manufacturing industry is therefore completely untenable.

Genuine monopolies can be established only by control of land or mineral resources. The notion that all the arable land on earth could be consolidated into a single world monopoly needs no further discussion; the only monopolies that we shall consider here are those originating in the control of useful minerals. Monopolies of this kind do, in fact, already exist in the case of a few minerals of minor importance, and it is at any rate conceivable that attempts to monopolize other minerals as well may some day prove successful. This would mean that the owners of such mines and quarries would derive an increased ground rent from them and that the consumers would restrict consumption and look for substitutes for the materials that had become more expensive. A world petroleum monopoly would lead to an increased demand for hydroelectric power, coal, etc. From the standpoint of world economy and *sub specie aeternitatis,* this would mean that we would have to be more sparing than we otherwise would have been in our use of those costly materials that we can only exhaust, but cannot replace, and thus leave more of them for future generations than would have been the case in an economy free of monopolies.

The bugbear of monopoly, which is always conjured up when one speaks of the unhampered development of the economy, need cause us no disquiet. The world monopolies that are really feasible could concern only a few items of primary production. Whether their effect is favorable or unfavorable cannot be so easily decided. In the eyes of those who, in treating economic problems, are unable to free themselves from feelings of envy, these monopolies appear as pernicious from the very fact that they yield their owners increased profits. Whoever approaches the question without prepossessions will find that such monopolies lead to a more sparing use of those mineral resources that are at man's disposal only in a rather limited quantity. If one really envies the monopolist his profit, one can, without danger and without having to expect any harmful economic consequences, have it pass into the public coffers by taxing the income from the mines.

In contradistinction to these world monopolies are the national and international monopolies, which are of practical importance today precisely because they do not originate in any natural evolutionary tendency on the part of the economic system when it is left to itself, but are the product of antiliberal economic policies. Attempts to secure a monopolistic position in regard to certain articles are in almost all cases feasible only because tariffs have divided the world market up into small national markets. Besides these, the only other cartels of any consequence are those which the owners of certain natural resources are able to form because the high cost of transportation protects them against the competition of producers from other areas in the narrow compass of their own locality.

It is a fundamental error, in judging the consequences of trusts, cartels, and enterprises supplying a market with one article alone, to speak of "control" of the market and of "price dictation" by the monopolist. The monopolist does not exercise any control, nor is he in a position to dictate prices. One could speak of control of the market or of price dictation only if the article in question were, in the strictest and most literal sense of the word, necessary for existence and absolutely irreplaceable by any substitute. This is evidently not true of any commodity. There is no economic good whose possession is indispensable to the existence of those prepared to purchase it on the market.

What distinguishes the formation of a monopoly price from the formation of a competitive price is the fact that, under certain very special conditions, it is possible for the monopolist to reap a greater profit from the sale of a smaller quantity at a higher price (which we call the monopoly price) than by selling at the price that the market would determine if more sellers were in competition (the competitive price). The special condition required for the emergence of a monopoly price is that the reaction of the consumers to a price increase does not involve a falling off of demand so sharp as to preclude a greater total profit from fewer sales at higher prices. If it is actually possible to achieve a monopolistic position in the market and to use it to realize monopoly prices, then profits higher than average will be yielded in the branch of industry concerned.

It may be that, in spite of these higher profits, new enterprises of the same kind are not undertaken because of the fear that, after reducing the monopoly price to the competitive price, they will not prove correspondingly profitable. One must, nevertheless, take into account the possibility that related industries, which are in a position to enter into production of the cartelized article at a relatively small cost, may appear as competitors; and, in any case, industries producing substitute commodities will be immediately at hand to avail themselves of the favorable circumstances for expanding their own production. All these factors make it extraordinarily rare for a monopoly to arise in a manufacturing industry that is not based on monopolistic control of particular raw materials. Where such monopolies do occur, they are always made possible only by certain legislative measures, such as patents and similar privileges, tariff regulations, tax laws, and the licensing system. A few decades ago people used to speak of a transportation monopoly. To what extent this monopoly was based on the licensing system remains uncertain. Today people generally do not bother much about it. The automobile and the airplane have become dangerous competitors of the railroads. But even before the appearance of these competitors the possibility of using waterways already set a definite limit to the rates that the railroads could venture to charge for their services on several lines.

It is not only a gross exaggeration, but a misunderstanding of the facts, to speak, as one commonly does today, of the formation of monopolies as having eliminated an essential prerequisite for the realization of the liberal ideal of a capitalist society. Twist and turn the monopoly problem as one may, one always comes back to the fact that monopoly prices are possible only where there is control over natural resources of a particular kind or where legislative enactments and their administration create the necessary conditions for the formation of monopolies. In the unhampered development of the economy, with the exception of mining and related branches of production, there is no tendency toward the exclusion of competition. The objection commonly raised against liberalism that the conditions of competition as they existed at the time when classical economics and liberal ideas were first developed no longer prevail is in no way justified. Only a few liberal demands (viz., free trade within and between nations) need to be realized in order to re-establish these conditions.

## 8. *Bureaucratization*

There is yet another sense in which it is commonly said that the necessary conditions for the realization of the liberal ideal of society no longer obtain today. In the big businesses made necessary by progress in the division of labor, the personnel employed must increase more and more. These enterprises must, therefore, in their conduct of business, become ever more like the government bureaucracy that the liberals in particular have made the target of their criticism. From day to day they become more cumbersome and less open to innovations. The selection of personnel for executive positions is no longer made on the basis of demonstrated proficiency on the job, but in accordance with purely formal criteria, such as educational background or seniority, and often just as a result of personal favoritism. Thus the distinctive feature of private, as opposed to public, enterprise finally disappears. If it was still justifiable in the age of classical liberalism to oppose government ownership on the ground that it paralyzes all free initiative and kills the joy of labor, it is no longer so today when private enterprises are carried on no less bureaucratically, pedantically, and formalistically than those that are publicly owned and operated.

In order to be able to assess the validity of these objections, one must first be clear as to what is really to be understood by bureaucracy and the bureaucratic conduct of business, and just how these are distinguished from commercial enterprise and the commercial conduct of business. The opposition between the commercial and the bureaucratic mentality is the counterpart in the intellectual realm of the opposition between capitalism—private ownership of the means of production—and socialism—communal ownership of the means of production. Whoever has factors of production at his disposal, whether his own or those lent to him by their owners in return for some compensation, must always be careful to employ them in such a way as to satisfy those needs of society that, under the given circumstances, are the most urgent. If he does not do this, he will operate at a loss and will find himself at first under the necessity of curtailing his activity as owner and entrepreneur and ultimately ousted from that position altogether. He ceases to be the one or the other and has to fall back into the ranks of those who have only their labor to sell and who do not have the responsibility of guiding production into those channels that, from the point of view of the consumers, are the right ones. In the calculation of profits and losses, which constitutes the whole sum and substance of the businessman's bookkeeping and accounting, entrepreneurs and capitalists possess a method that enables them to check, with the greatest attainable exactitude, every step in their procedure down to the smallest detail and, where possible, to see what effect each individual transaction in the conduct of their operations will have on the total outcome of the enterprise. Monetary calculation and cost accounting constitute the most important intellectual tool of the capitalist entrepreneur, and it was no one less than Goethe who pronounced the system of double-entry bookkeeping "one of the finest inventions of the human mind." Goethe could say this because he was free from the resentment that the petty literati always foster against the businessman. It is they that form the chorus whose constant refrain is that monetary calculation and concern with profit and loss are the most shameful of sins.

Monetary calculation, bookkeeping, and statistics on sales and operations make it possible for even the biggest and most complex business concerns to make an exact check on the results achieved in every single department and thereby to form a judgment on the extent to which the head of each department has contributed to the total success of the enterprise. Thus, a reliable guide is provided for determining the treatment to be accorded to the managers of the various departments. One can know what they are worth and how much they are to be paid. Advancement to higher and more responsible positions is by way of unquestionably demonstrated success in a more circumscribed sphere of action. And just as one is able to check on the activity of the manager of each department by means of cost accounting, so one can also scrutinize the activity of the enterprise in every single field of its over-all operation, as well as the effects of certain organizational and similar measures.

There are, to be sure, limits to this exact control. One cannot determine the success or failure of the activity of each individual within a department as one can that of its manager. There are, besides, departments whose contribution to the total output cannot be comprehended by means of calculation: what a research department, a legal bureau, a secretariat, a statistical service, etc., accomplishes cannot be ascertained in the same way as, for instance, the performance of a particular sales or production department. The former may be quite safely left to the approximate estimation of the person in charge of the department, and the latter to that of the general manager of the concern; for conditions can be seen with relative clarity and those who are called upon to make these judgments (both the general manage-ment and that of the various departments) have a personal interest in their correctness, as their own incomes are affected by the productivity of the operations of which they are in charge.

The opposite of this type of enterprise, whose every transaction is controlled by the calculation of profit and loss, is represented by the apparatus of public administration. Whether a judge (and what is true of a judge is true in the same way of every high administrative official) has discharged his duties better or worse cannot be demonstrated by any computation. There is no possible way of establishing by an objective criterion whether a district or a province is being administered well or badly, cheaply or expensively. The judgment of the activity of public officials is thus a matter of subjective, and therefore quite arbitrary, opinion. Even the question whether a particular bureau is necessary, whether it has too many or too few employees, and whether its organization is or is not suited to its purpose can be decided only on the basis of considerations that involve some element of subjectivity. There is but one field of public administration in which the criterion of success or failure is unquestionable: the waging of war. But even here the only thing certain is whether the operation has been crowned with success. The question how far the distribution of power determined the issue even before the beginning of hostilities and how much of the outcome is to be attributed to the competence or incompetence of the leaders in their conduct of the operations and to the appropriateness of the measures they took cannot be strictly and precisely answered. There have been generals celebrated for their victories who, in fact, did everything to facilitate the triumph of the enemy and who owe their success solely to circumstances so favorable as to outweigh their mistakes. And vanquished leaders have sometimes been condemned whose genius had done everything possible to prevent the inevitable defeat.

The manager of a private enterprise gives the employees to whom he assigns independent duties only one directive: to make as much profit as possible. Everything that he has to say to them is comprehended in this one order, and an examination of the accounts makes it possible to determine easily and accurately to what extent they have followed it. The manager of a bureaucratic department finds himself in a quite different situation. He can tell his subordinates what they have to accomplish, but he is not in a position to ascertain whether the means employed for the attainment of this result are the most appropriate and economical under the circumstances. If he is not omnipresent in all the offices and bureaus subordinate to him, he cannot judge whether the attainment of the same result would not have been possible with a lesser expenditure of labor and materials. The fact that the result itself is also not amenable to numerical measurement, but only to approximate assessment, need not be discussed here. For we are not considering administrative technique from the point of view of its external effects, but merely from the standpoint of its reaction upon the internal operation of the bureaucratic apparatus; we are concerned with the result attained, therefore, only in its relation to the expenses incurred.

Because it is out of the question to undertake to determine this relationship by means of computations after the manner of commercial bookkeeping, the manager of a bureaucratic organization must provide his subordinates with instructions with which compliance is made obligatory. In these instructions provision is made, in a general way, for the ordinary and regular course of business. In all extraordinary cases, however, before any money is spent, permission must first be obtained from higher authority —a tedious and rather ineffectual procedure in favor of which all that can be said is that it is the only method possible. For if every subaltern bureau, every department head, every branch office, were given the right to make the expenditures that they deemed requisite, the costs of administration would soon soar without limit. One should not delude oneself about the fact that this system is seriously defective and very unsatisfactory. Many expenses are incurred that are superfluous, and many that would be necessary are not made because a bureaucratic apparatus cannot, by its very nature, adjust itself to circumstances as a commercial organization can.

The effect of bureaucratization is most apparent in its representative—the bureaucrat. In a private enterprise, the hiring of labor is not the conferring of a favor, but a business transaction from which both parties, employer and employee, benefit. The employer must endeavor to pay wages corresponding in value to the labor performed. If he does not do this, he runs the risk of seeing the worker leave his employment for that of a better-paying competitor. The employee, in order not to lose his job, must in his turn endeavor to fulfill the duties of his position well enough to be worth his wages. Since employment is not a favor, but a business transaction, the employee does not need to fear that he may be discharged if he falls into personal disfavor. For the entrepreneur who discharges, for reasons of personal bias, a useful employee who is worth his pay harms only himself and not the worker, who can find a similar position elsewhere. There is not the slightest difficulty in entrusting to the manager of each department the authority to hire and fire employees; for under the pressure of the control exercised over his activities by bookkeeping and cost accounting he must see to it that his department shows as great a profit as possible, and hence he is obliged, in his own interest, to be careful to retain the best employees there. If out of spite he discharges someone whom he ought not to have discharged, if his actions are motivated by personal, and not objective, considerations, then it is he himself who must suffer the consequences. Any impairment of the success of the department headed by him must ultimately redound to his loss. Thus, the incorporation of the nonmaterial factor, labor, into the process of production takes place without any friction.

In a bureaucratic organization things are quite different. Since the productive contribution of the individual department, and hence also of the individual employee, even when he occupies an executive position, cannot in this case be ascertained, the door is wide open to favoritism and personal bias both in appointment and remuneration. The fact that the intercession of influential persons plays a certain role in filling official positions in the civil service is not due to a peculiar baseness of character on the part of those responsible for filling these posts, but to the fact that from the very outset there is no objective criterion for determining an individual's qualification for appointment. Of course, it is the most competent who ought to be employed, but the question is: Who is the most competent? If this question could be as easily answered as the question what an ironworker or a compositor is worth, there would be no problem. But since this is not the case, an element of arbitrariness is necessarily involved in comparing the qualifications of different individuals.

In order to keep this within the narrowest possible limits, one seeks to set up formal conditions for appointment and promotion. Attainment to a particular position is made dependent on the fulfillment of certain educational requirements, on the passing of examinations, and on continued employment for a certain period of time in other positions; promotion is made dependent on years of previous service. Naturally, all these expedients are in no sense a substitute for the possibility of finding the best available man for every post by means of the calculation of profit and loss. It would be supererogatory to point out in particular that attendance at school, examinations, and seniority do not offer the slightest guarantee that the selection will be correct. On the contrary: this system from the very outset prevents the energetic and the competent from occupying positions in line with their powers and capabilities. Never yet has anyone of real worth risen to the top by way of a prescribed program of study and promotion in due course along the established lines. Even in Germany, which has a pious faith in her bureaucrats, the expression, "a perfect functionary," is used to connote a spineless and ineffectual person, however well intentioned.

Thus, the characteristic mark of bureaucratic management is that it lacks the guidance provided by considerations of profit and loss in judging the success of its operations in relation to the expenses incurred and is consequently obliged, in the effort to compensate for this deficiency, to resort to the entirely inadequate expedient of making its conduct of affairs and the hiring of its personnel subject to a set of formal prescriptions. All the evils that are commonly imputed to bureaucratic management—its inflexibility, its lack of resourcefulness, and its helplessness in the face of problems that are easily solved in profit-seeking enterprise —are the result of this one fundamental deficiency. As long as the activity of the state is restricted to the narrow field that liberalism assigns to it, the disadvantages of bureaucracy cannot, at any rate, make themselves too apparent. They become a grave problem for the whole economy only when the state—and naturally the same is true of municipalities and other forms of local government—proceeds to socialize the means of production and to take an active part in it or even in trade.

A public enterprise conducted with an eye to maximizing profits can, to be sure, make use of monetary calculation as long as most business is privately owned and hence a market still exists and market prices are formed. The only hindrance to its operation and development is the fact that its managers, as functionaries of the state, do not have the personal interest in the success or failure of the business that is characteristic of the management of private enterprises. The director cannot, therefore, be given freedom to act independently in making crucial decisions. Since he would not suffer the losses that could result, under certain circumstances, from his business policy, his conduct of affairs could all too easily be disposed to run risks that would not be taken by a director who, because he must share in the loss, is genuinely responsible. His authority must, therefore, be in some way limited. Whether it is bound by a set of rigid regulations or the decisions of a control council or the consent of a superior authority, bureaucratic management in any case continues to suffer from the unwieldiness and the lack of ability to adjust itself to changing conditions that have everywhere led public enterprises from one failure to another.

But, in fact, it is only seldom that a public enterprise aims at nothing but profit and sets aside all other considerations. As a rule, it is demanded of a public enterprise that it keep in mind certain "national" and other considerations. It is expected, for instance, in its procurement and sales policy, to favor domestic as against foreign production. It is demanded of state railways that they set a schedule of rates that will serve a specific commercial policy on the part of the government, that they construct and maintain lines that cannot be profitably operated simply in order to promote the economic development of a certain area, and that they operate certain others for strategic or similar reasons. When such factors play a role in the conduct of a business, all control by the methods of cost accounting and the calculation of profit and loss is out of the question. The director of the state railways who presents an unfavorable balance sheet at the end of the year is in a position to say: "The railway lines under my supervision have, to be sure, operated at a loss if considered from the strictly commercial point of view of profit-seeking private enterprise; but if one takes into consideration such factors as our national economic and military policy, one must not forget that they have accomplished a great deal that does not enter into the calculation of profit and loss." Under such circumstances the calculation of profit and loss has clearly lost all value for judging the success of an enterprise, so that—even apart from other factors having the same tendency—it must necessarily be managed quite as bureaucratically as, for example, the administration of a prison or a tax bureau.

No private enterprise, whatever its size, can ever become bureaucratic as long as it is entirely and solely operated on a profit basis. Firm adherence to the entrepreneurial principle of aiming at the highest profit makes it possible for even the largest concern to ascertain with complete precision the part played by every transaction and by the activity of every department in contributing to the total result. As long as enterprises look only to profit, they are proof against all the evils of bureaucratism. The bureaucratization of privately owned enterprises that we see going on about us everywhere today is purely the result of interventionism, which forces them to take into account factors that, if they were free to determine their policies for themselves, would be far from playing any role whatsoever in the conduct of their business. When a concern must pay heed to political prejudices and sensibilities of all kinds in order to avoid being continually harassed by various organs of the state, it soon finds that it is no longer in a position to base its calculations on the solid ground of profit and loss. For instance, some of the public utility enterprises in the United States, in order to avoid conflicts with public opinion and with the legislative, judicial, and administrative organs of the government which it influences, make it a policy not to hire Catholics, Jews, atheists, Darwinists, Negroes, Irishmen, Germans, Italians, and all newly arrived immigrants. In the interventionist state, every business is under the necessity of accommodating itself to the wishes of the authorities in order to avoid burdensome penalties. The result is that these and other considerations foreign to the profit-seeking principle of entrepreneurial management come to play an ever increasing role in the conduct of business, while the part played by precise calculation and cost accounting concomitantly dwindles in significance, and private enterprise begins increasingly to adopt the mode of management of public enterprises, with their elaborate apparatus of formally prescribed rules and regulations. In a word, it becomes bureaucratized.

Thus, the progressing bureaucratization of big business is by no means the result of an inexorable tendency inherent in the development of the capitalist economy. It is nothing but the necessary consequence of adopting a policy of interventionism. In the absence of government interference with their operations, even the largest firms could be run in exactly as businesslike a way as the small ones.

# 3

# Liberal Foreign Policy

## 1. *The Boundaries of the State*

For the liberal, there is no opposition between domestic policy and foreign policy, and the question so often raised and exhaustively discussed, whether considerations of foreign policy take precedence over those of domestic policy or *vice versa*, is, in his eyes, an idle one. For liberalism is, from the very outset, a world-embracing political concept, and the same ideas that it seeks to realize within a limited area it holds to be valid also for the larger sphere of world politics. If the liberal makes a distinction between domestic and foreign policy, he does so solely for purposes of convenience and classification, to subdivide the vast domain of political problems into major types, and not because he is of the opinion that different principles are valid for each.

The goal of the domestic policy of liberalism is the same as that of its foreign policy: peace. It aims at peaceful cooperation just as much between nations as within each nation. The starting-point of liberal thought is the recognition of the value and importance of human cooperation, and the whole policy and program of liberalism is designed to serve the purpose of maintaining the existing state of mutual cooperation among the members of the human race and of extending it still further. The ultimate ideal envisioned by liberalism is the perfect cooperation of all mankind, taking place peacefully and without friction. Liberal thinking always has the whole of humanity in view and

105

not just parts. It does not stop at limited groups; it does not end at the border of the village, of the province, of the nation, or of the continent. Its thinking is cosmopolitan and ecumenical: it takes in all men and the whole world. Liberalism is, in this sense, humanism; and the liberal, a citizen of the world, a cosmopolite.

Today, when the world is dominated by antiliberal ideas, cosmopolitanism is suspect in the eyes of the masses. In Germany there are overzealous patriots who cannot forgive the great German poets, especially Goethe, whose thinking and feeling, instead of being confined by national bounds, had a cosmopolitan orientation. It is thought that an irreconcilable conflict exists between the interests of the nation and those of mankind and that one who directs his aspirations and endeavors toward the welfare of the whole of humanity thereby disregards the interests of his own nation. No belief could be more deeply mistaken. The German who works for the good of all mankind no more injures the particular interests of his compatriots—i.e., those of his fellow men with whom he shares a common land and language and with whom he often forms an ethnic and spiritual community as well—than one who works for the good of the whole German nation injures the interests of his own home town. For the individual has just as much of an interest in the prosperity of the whole world as he has in the blooming and flourishing of the local community in which he lives.

The chauvinistic nationalists, who maintain that irreconcilable conflicts of interests exist among the various nations and who seek the adoption of a policy aimed at securing, by force if need be, the supremacy of their own nation over all others, are generally most emphatic in insisting on the necessity and utility of internal national unity. The greater the stress they place on the necessity of war against foreign nations, the more urgently do they call for peace and concord among the members of their own nation. Now this demand for domestic unity the liberal by no means opposes. On the contrary: the demand for peace within each nation was itself an outcome of liberal thinking and attained to prominence only as the liberal ideas of the eighteenth century came to be more widely accepted. Before the liberal philosophy, with its unconditional extolment of peace, gained ascendancy over men's minds, the waging of war was not confined to conflicts between one country and another. Nations were themselves torn by continual civil strife and sanguinary internal struggles. In the eighteenth century Briton still stood arrayed in battle against Briton at Culloden, and even as late as the nineteenth century, in Germany, while Prussia waged war against Austria, other German states joined in the fighting on both sides. At that time Prussia saw nothing wrong in fighting on the side of Italy against German Austria, and, in 1870, only the rapid progress of events prevented Austria from joining the French in the war against Prussia and its allies. Many of the victories of which the Prussian army is so proud were won by Prussian troops over those of other German states. It was liberalism that first taught the nations to preserve in their internal conduct of affairs the peace that it desires to teach them to keep also in their relations with other countries.

It is from the fact of the international division of labor that liberalism derives the decisive, irrefutable argument against war. The division of labor has for a long time now gone beyond the boundaries of any one nation. No civilized nation today satisfies its need as a self-sufficient community directly from its own production. All are obliged to obtain goods from abroad and to pay for them by exporting domestic products. Anything that would have the effect of preventing or stopping the international exchange of goods would do immense damage to the whole of human civilization and undermine the well-being, indeed, the very basis of existence, of millions upon millions of people. In an age in which nations are mutually dependent on products of foreign provenance, wars can no longer be waged. Since any stoppage in the flow of imports could have a decisive effect on the outcome of a war waged by a nation involved in the international division of labor, a policy that wishes to take into consideration the possibility of a war must endeavor to make the national economy self-sufficient, i.e., it must, even in time of peace, aim at making the international division of labor come to an end at its own borders. If Germany wished to withdraw from the international division of labor and attempted to satisfy all its needs directly through domestic production, the total annual product of German labor would diminish, and thus the well-being, the standard of living, and the cultural level of the German people would decline considerably.

## 2. The Right of Self-Determination

It has already been pointed out that a country can enjoy domestic peace only when a democratic constitution provides the guarantee that the adjustment of the government to the will of the citizens can take place without friction. Nothing else is required than the consistent application of the same principle in order to assure international peace as well.

The liberals of an earlier age thought that the peoples of the world were peaceable by nature and that only monarchs desire war in order to increase their power and wealth by the conquest of provinces. They believed, therefore, that to assure lasting peace it was sufficient to replace the rule of dynastic princes by governments dependent on the people. If a democratic republic finds that its existing boundaries, as shaped by the course of history before the transition to liberalism, no longer correspond to the political wishes of the people, they must be peacefully changed to conform to the results of a plebiscite expressing the people's will. It must always be possible to shift the boundaries of the state if the will of the inhabitants of an area to attach themselves to a state other than the one to which they presently belong has made itself clearly known. In the seventeenth and eighteenth centuries, the Russian Czars incorporated into their empire large areas whose population had never felt the desire to belong to the Russian state. Even if the Russian Empire had adopted a completely democratic constitution, the wishes of the inhabitants of these territories would not have been satisfied, because they simply did not desire to associate themselves in any bond of political union with the Russians. Their democratic demand was: freedom from the Russian Empire; the formation of an independent Poland, Finland, Latvia, Lithuania, etc. The fact that these demands and similar ones on the part of other peoples (e.g., the Italians, the Germans in Schleswig-Holstein, the Slavs in the Hapsburg Empire) could be satisfied only by recourse to arms was the most important cause of all the wars that have been fought in Europe since the Congress of Vienna.

The right of self-determination in regard to the question of membership in a state thus means: whenever the inhabitants of a particular territory, whether it be a single village, a whole district, or a series of adjacent districts, make it known, by a freely conducted plebiscite, that they no longer wish to remain united to the state to which they belong at the time, but wish either to form an independent state or to attach themselves to some other state, their wishes are to be respected and complied with. This is the only feasible and effective way of preventing revolutions and civil and international wars.

To call this right of self-determination the "right of self-determination of nations" is to misunderstand it. It is not the right of self-determination of a delimited national unit, but the right of the inhabitants of every territory to decide on the state to which they wish to belong. This misunderstanding is even more grievous when the expression "self-determination of nations" is taken to mean that a national state has the right to detach and incorporate into itself against the will of the inhabitants parts of the nation that belong to the territory of another state. It is in terms of the right of self-determination of nations understood in this sense that the Italian Fascists seek to justify their demand that the canton Tessin and parts of other cantons be detached from Switzerland and united to Italy, even though the inhabitants of these cantons have no such desire. A similar position is taken by some of the advocates of Pan-Germanism in regard to German Switzerland and the Netherlands.

However, the right of self-determination of which we speak is not the right of self-determination of nations, but rather the right of self-determination of the inhabitants of every territory large enough to form an independent administrative unit. If it were in any way possible to grant this right of self-determination to every individual person, it would have to be done. This is impracticable only because of compelling technical considerations, which make it necessary that a region be governed as a single administrative unit and that the right of self-determination be restricted to the will of the majority of the inhabitants of areas large enough to count as territorial units in the administration of the country.

So far as the right of self-determination was given effect at all, and wherever it would have been permitted to take effect, in the nineteenth and twentieth centuries, it led or would have led to the formation of states composed of a single nationality (i.e., people speaking the same language) and to the dissolution of states composed of several nationalities, but only as a consequence of the free choice of those entitled to participate in the plebiscite. The formation of states comprising all the members of a national group was the *result* of the exercise of the right of self-determination, not its purpose. If some members of a nation feel happier politically independent than as a part of a state composed of all the members of the same linguistic group, one may, of course, attempt to change their political ideas by persuasion in order to win them over to the principle of nationality, according to which all members of the same linguistic group should form a single, independent state. If, however, one seeks to determine their political fate against their will by appealing to an alleged higher right of the nation, one violates the right of self-determination no less effectively than by practicing any other form of oppression. A partition of Switzerland among Germany, France, and Italy, even if it were performed exactly according to linguistic boundaries, would be just as gross a violation of the right of self-determination as was the partition of Poland.

## 3. The Political Foundations of Peace

One would think that after the experience of the World War the realization of the necessity of perpetual peace would have become increasingly common. However, it is still not appreciated

that everlasting peace can be achieved only by putting the liberal
program into effect generally and holding to it constantly and
consistently and that the World War was nothing but the natural
and necessary consequence of the antiliberal policies of the last
decades.

A senseless and thoughtless slogan makes capitalism responsible
for the origin of the war. The connection between the latter and
the policy of protectionism is clearly evident, and, as a result of
what is certainly a grievous ignorance of the facts, the protective
tariff is identified outright with capitalism. People forget that
only a short time ago all the nationalistic publications were filled
with violent diatribes against international capital ("finance capital" and the "international gold trust") for being without a
country, for opposing protective tariffs, for being averse to war
and inclined toward peace. It is altogether absurd to hold the
armaments industry responsible for the outbreak of the war. The
armaments industry has arisen and grown to a considerable size
because governments and peoples bent on war demanded
weapons. It would be really preposterous to suppose that the
nations turned to imperialistic policies as a favor to the ordnance
manufacturers. The armaments industry, like every other, arose
in order to satisfy a demand. If the nations had preferred other
things to bullets and explosives, then the factory-owners would
have produced the former instead of the materials of war.

One can assume that the desire for peace is today universal.
But the peoples of the world are not at all clear as to what
conditions would have to be fulfilled in order to secure peace.

If the peace is not to be disturbed, all incentive for aggression
must be eliminated. A world order must be established in which
nations and national groups are so satisfied with living conditions
that they will not feel impelled to resort to the desperate expedient of war. The liberal does not expect to abolish war by preach-
ing and moralizing. He seeks to create the social conditions that
will eliminate the causes of war.

The first requirement in this regard is private property. When
private property must be respected even in time of war, when
the victor is not entitled to appropriate to himself the property

of private persons, and the appropriation of public property has no great significance because private ownership of the means of production prevails everywhere, an important motive for waging war has already been excluded. However, this is far from being enough to guarantee peace. So that the exercise of the right of self-determination may not be reduced to a farce, political institutions must be such as to render the transference of sovereignty over a territory from one government to another a matter of the least possible significance, involving no advantage or disadvantage for anyone. People do not have a correct conception of what this requires. It is therefore necessary to make it clear by a few examples.

Examine a map of linguistic and national groups in Central or Eastern Europe and notice how often, for example, in northern and western Bohemia, boundaries between them are crossed by railway lines. Here, under conditions of interventionism and etatism, there is no way of making the borders of the state correspond to the linguistic frontier. It will not do to operate a Czech state railroad on the soil of the German state, and it will do even less to run a railroad line that is under a different management every few miles. It would be just as unthinkable after every few minutes or quarter of an hour on a railroad trip to have to face a tariff barrier with all its formalities. It is thus easy to understand why etatists and interventionists reach the conclusion that the "geographic" or "economic" unity of such areas must not be "ruptured" and that the territory in question must therefore be placed under the sovereignty of a single "ruler." (Obviously, every nation seeks to prove that it alone is entitled and competent to play the role of ruler under such circumstances.) For liberalism there is no problem here at all. Private railroads, if quite free of government interference, can traverse the territory of many states without any trouble. If there are no tariff boundaries and no limitations on the movement of persons, animals, or goods, then it is of no consequence whether a train ride in a few hours crosses over the borders of the state more or less often.

The linguistic map also reveals the existence of national enclaves. Without any land connection of the same nationality with the main body of their people, compatriots dwell together in closed-off settlements or linguistic islands. Under present political conditions, they cannot be incorporated into the mother country. The fact that the area encompassed by the state is today protected by tariff walls makes unbroken territorial continuity a political necessity. A small "foreign possession," in being isolated from the immediately adjacent territory by tariffs and other measures of protectionism, would be exposed to economic strangulation. But once there is free trade and the state restricts itself to the preservation of private property, nothing is simpler than the solution of this problem. No linguistic island then has to acquiesce in the infringement of its rights as a nation merely because it is not connected to the main body of its own people by a territorial bridge inhabited by its fellow nationals.

The notorious "problem of the corridor" also arises only in an imperialist-etatist-interventionist system. An inland country believes that it needs a "corridor" to the sea in order to keep its foreign trade free of the influence of the interventionist and etatist policies of the countries whose territories separate it from the sea. If free trade were the rule, it would be hard to see what advantage an inland country could expect from the possession of a "corridor."

Transfer from one "economic zone" (in the etatist sense) to another has serious economic consequences. One need only think, for instance, of the cotton industry of upper Alsatia, which has twice had to undergo this experience, or the Polish textile industry of Upper Silesia, etc. If a change in the political affiliation of a territory involves advantages or disadvantages for its inhabitants, then their freedom to vote for the state to which they really wish to belong is essentially limited. One can speak of genuine self-determination only if the decision of each individual stems from his own free will, and not from fear of loss or hope of profit. A capitalist world organized on liberal principles knows no separate "economic" zones. In such a world, the whole of the earth's surface forms a single economic territory.

The right of self-determination works to the advantage only of those who comprise the majority. In order to protect minorities as well, domestic measures are required, of which we shall first consider those involving the national policy in regard to education.

In most countries today school attendance, or at least private instruction, is compulsory. Parents are obliged to send their children to school for a certain number of years or, in lieu of this public instruction at school, to have them given equivalent instruction at home. It is pointless to go into the reasons that were advanced for and against compulsory education when the matter was still a live issue. They do not have the slightest relevance to the problem as it exists today. There is only *one* argument that has any bearing at all on this question, viz., that continued adherence to a policy of compulsory education is utterly incompatible with efforts to establish lasting peace.

The inhabitants of London, Paris, and Berlin will no doubt find such a statement completely incredible. What in the world does compulsory education have to do with war and peace? One must not, however, judge this question, as one does so many others, exclusively from the point of view of the peoples of Western Europe. In London, Paris, and Berlin, the problem of compulsory education is, to be sure, easily solved. In these cities no doubt can arise as to which language is to be used in giving instruction. The population that lives in these cities and sends its children to school may be considered, by and large, of homogeneous nationality. But even the non-English-speaking people who live in London find it in the obvious interest of their children that instruction is given in English and in no other language, and things are not different in Paris and Berlin.

However, the problem of compulsory education has an entirely different significance in those extensive areas in which peoples speaking different languages live together side by side and intermingled in polyglot confusion. Here the question of which language is to be made the basis of instruction assumes crucial importance. A decision one way or the other can, over the years, determine the nationality of a whole area. The school can alienate children from the nationality to which their parents belong and can be used as a means of oppressing whole nationalities. Whoever controls the schools has the power to injure other nationalities and to benefit his own.

It is no solution of this problem to suggest that each child be sent to the school in which the language of his parents is spoken. First of all, even apart from the problem posed by children of mixed linguistic background, it is not always easy to decide what the language of the parents is. In polyglot areas many persons are required by their profession to make use of all the languages spoken in the country. Besides, it is often not possible for an individual—again out of regard for his means of livelihood—to declare himself openly for one or another nationality. Under a system of interventionism, it could cost him the patronage of customers belonging to other nationalities or a job with an entrepreneur of a different nationality. Then again, there are many parents who would even prefer to send their children to the schools of another nationality than their own because they value the advantages of bilingualism or assimilation to the other nationality more highly than loyalty to their own people. If one leaves to the parents the choice of the school to which they wish to send their children, then one exposes them to every conceivable form of political coercion. In all areas of mixed nationality, the school is a political prize of the highest importance. It cannot be deprived of its political character as long as it remains a public and compulsory institution. There is, in fact, only *one* solution: the state, the government, the laws must not in any way concern themselves with schooling or education. Public funds must not be used for such purposes. The rearing and instruction of youth must be left entirely to parents and to private associations and institutions.

It is better that a number of boys grow up without formal education than that they enjoy the benefit of schooling only to run the risk, once they have grown up, of being killed or maimed. A healthy illiterate is always better than a literate cripple.

But even if we eliminate the spiritual coercion exercised by compulsory education, we should still be far from having done everything that is necessary in order to remove all the sources of friction between the nationalities living in polyglot territories.

The school is one means of oppressing nationalities—perhaps the most dangerous, in our opinion—but it certainly is not the only means. Every interference on the part of the government in economic life can become a means of persecuting the members of nationalities speaking a language different from that of the ruling group. For this reason, in the interest of preserving peace, the activity of the government must be limited to the sphere in which it is, in the strictest sense of the word, indispensable.

We cannot do without the apparatus of government in protecting and preserving the life, liberty, property, and health of the individual. But even the judicial and police activities performed in the service of these ends can become dangerous in areas where any basis at all can be found for discriminating between one group and another in the conduct of official business. Only in countries where there is no particular incentive for partiality will there generally be no reason to fear that a magistrate who is supposed to apply the established laws for the protection of life, liberty, property, and health will act in a biased manner. Where, however, differences of religion, nationality, or the like have divided the population into groups separated by a gulf so deep as to exclude every impulse of fairness or humanity and to leave room for nothing but hate, the situation is quite different. Then the judge who acts consciously, or still more often unconsciously, in a biased manner thinks he is fulfilling a higher duty when he makes use of the prerogatives and powers of his office in the service of his own group.

To the extent that the apparatus of government has no other function than that of protecting life, liberty, property, and health, it is possible, at any rate, to draw up regulations that so strictly circumscribe the domain in which the administrative authorities and the courts are free to act as to leave little or no latitude for the exercise of their own discretion or arbitrary, subjective judgment. But once a share in the management of production is relinquished to the state, once the apparatus of government is called upon to determine the disposition of goods of higher order, it is impossible to hold administrative officials to a set of binding rules and regulations that would guarantee certain rights to every citizen. A penal law designed to punish murderers can, to some extent at least, draw a dividing line between what is and what is not to be considered murder and thus set certain limits to the area in which the magistrate is free to use his own judgment. Of course, every lawyer knows only too well that even the best law can be perverted, in concrete cases, in interpretation, application, and administration. But in the case of a government bureau charged with the management of transportation facilities, mines, or public lands, as much as one may restrain its freedom of action on other grounds (which have already been discussed in section 2), the most one can do to keep it impartial in regard to controversial questions of national policy is to give it directives couched in empty generalities. One must grant it a great deal of leeway in many respects because one cannot know beforehand under what circumstances it will have to act. Thus, the door is left wide open for arbitrariness, bias, and the abuse of official power.

Even in areas inhabited by people of various nationalities, there is need for a unified administration. One cannot place at every street-corner both a German and a Czech policeman, each of whom would have to protect only members of his own nationality. And even if this could be done, the question would still arise as to who is to intervene when members of both nationalities are involved in a situation that calls for intervention. The disadvantages that result from the necessity of a unified administration in these territories are unavoidable. But if difficulties already exist even in carrying out such indispensable functions of government as the protection of life, liberty, property, and health, one should not raise them to really monstrous proportions by extending the range of state activity to other fields in which, by their very nature, still greater latitude must be granted to arbitrary judgment.

Large areas of the world have been settled, not by the members of just one nationality, one race, or one religion, but by a motley mixture of many peoples. As a result of the migratory movements that necessarily follow shifts in the location of production, more new territories are continually being confronted with the problem of a mixed population. If one does not wish to aggravate artificially the friction that must arise from this living together of different groups, one must restrict the state to just those tasks that it alone can perform.

## 4. Nationalism

As long as nations were ruled by monarchical despots, the idea of adjusting the boundaries of the state to coincide with the boundaries between nationalities could not find acceptance. If a potentate desired to incorporate a province into his realm, he cared little whether the inhabitants—the subjects—agreed to a change of rulers or not. The only consideration that was regarded as relevant was whether the available military forces were sufficient to conquer and hold the territory in question. One justified one's conduct publicly by the more or less artificial construction of a legal claim. The nationality of the inhabitants of the area concerned was not taken into account at all.

It was with the rise of liberalism that the question of how the boundaries of states are to be drawn first became a problem independent of military, historical, and legal considerations. Liberalism, which founds the state on the will of the majority of the people living in a certain territory, disallows all military considerations that were formerly decisive in defining the boundaries of the state. It rejects the right of conquest. It cannot understand how people can speak of "strategic frontiers" and finds entirely incomprehensible the demand that a piece of land be incorporated into one's own state in order to possess a glacis. Liberalism does not acknowledge the historical right of a prince to inherit a province. A king can rule, in the liberal sense, only over persons and not over a certain piece of land, of which the inhabitants are viewed as mere appendages. The monarch by the grace of God carries the title of a territory, e.g., "King of France." The kings installed by liberalism received their title, not from the name of the territory, but from that of the people over whom they ruled as constitutional monarchs. Thus, Louis Philippe bore the title, "King of the French"; thus too, there is a "King of the Belgians," as there was once a "King of the Hellenes."

It was liberalism that created the legal form by which the desire of the people to belong or not to belong to a certain state could gain expression, viz., the plebiscite. The state to which the inhabitants of a certain territory wish to belong is to be ascertained by means of an election. But even if all the necessary economic and political conditions (e.g., those involving the national policy in regard to education) were fulfilled in order to prevent the plebiscite from being reduced to a farce, even if it were possible simply to take a poll of the inhabitants of every community in order to determine to which state they wished to attach themselves, and to repeat such an election whenever circumstances changed, some unresolved problems would certainly still remain as possible sources of friction between the different nationalities. The situation of having to belong to a state to which one does not wish to belong is no less onerous if it is the result of an election than if one must endure it as the consequence of a military conquest. But it is doubly difficult for the individual who is cut off from the majority of his fellow citizens by a language barrier.

To be a member of a national minority always means that one is a second-class citizen. Discussions of political questions must, of course, be carried on by means of the written and spoken word —in speeches, newspaper articles, and books. However, these means of political enlightenment and debate are not at the disposal of the linguistic minority to the same extent as they are for those whose mother tongue—the language used in everyday speech—is that in which the discussions take place. The political thought of a people, after all, is the reflection of the ideas contained in its political literature. Cast into the form of statute law, the outcome of its political discussions acquires direct significance for the citizen who speaks a foreign tongue, since he must obey the law; yet he has the feeling that he is excluded from effective participation in shaping the will of the legislative authority or at least that he is not allowed to cooperate in shaping it to the same extent as those whose native tongue is that of the ruling majority. And when he appears before a magistrate or any administrative official as a party to a suit or a petition, he stands before men whose political thought is foreign to him because it developed under different ideological influences.

But even apart from all this, the very fact that the members of the minority are required, in appearing before tribunals and administrative authorities, to make use of a language foreign to them already handicaps them seriously in many respects. There is all the difference in the world, when one is on trial, between being able to speak in court directly to one's judges and being compelled to avail oneself of the services of an interpreter. At every turn, the member of a national minority is made to feel that he lives among strangers and that he is, even if the letter of the law denies it, a second-class citizen.

All these disadvantages are felt to be very oppressive even in a state with a liberal constitution in which the activity of the government is restricted to the protection of the life and property of the citizens. But they become quite intolerable in an interventionist or a socialist state. If the administrative authorities have the right to intervene everywhere according to their free discretion, if the latitude granted to judges and officials in reaching their decisions is so wide as to leave room also for the operation of political prejudices, then a member of a national minority finds himself delivered over to arbitrary judgment and oppression on the part of the public functionaries belonging to the ruling majority. What happens when school and church as well are not independent, but subject to regulation by the government, has already been discussed.

It is here that one must seek for the roots of the aggressive nationalism that we see at work today. Efforts to trace back to natural rather than political causes the violent antagonisms existing between nations today are altogether mistaken. All the symptoms of supposedly innate antipathy between peoples that are customarily offered in evidence exist also within each individual nation. The Bavarian hates the Prussian; the Prussian, the Bavarian. No less fierce is the hatred existing among individual groups within both France and Poland. Nevertheless, Germans, Poles, and Frenchmen manage to live peacefully within their own countries. What gives the antipathy of the Pole for the German and of the German for the Pole a special political significance is the aspiration of each of the two peoples to seize for itself political control of the border areas in which Germans and Poles live side by side and to use it to oppress the members of the other nationality. What has kindled the hatred between nations to a consuming fire is the fact that people want to use the schools to estrange children from the language of their fathers and to make use of the courts and administrative offices, political and economic measures, and outright expropriation to persecute those speaking a foreign tongue. Because people are prepared to resort to violent means in order to create favorable conditions for the political future of their own nation, they have established a system of oppression in the polyglot areas that imperils the peace of the world.

As long as the liberal program is not completely carried out in the territories of mixed nationality, hatred between members of different nations must become ever fiercer and continue to ignite new wars and rebellions.

### 5. *Imperialism*

The lust for conquest on the part of the absolute monarchs of previous centuries was aimed at an extension of their sphere of power and an increase in their wealth. No prince could be powerful enough, for it was by force alone that he could preserve his rule against internal and external enemies. No prince could be rich enough, for he needed money for the maintenance of his soldiers and the upkeep of his entourage.

For a liberal state, the question whether or not the boundaries of its territory are to be further extended is of minor significance. Wealth cannot be won by the annexation of new provinces, since the "revenue" derived from a territory must be used to defray the necessary costs of its administration. For a liberal state, which entertains no aggressive plans, a strengthening of its military power is unimportant. Thus, liberal parliaments resisted all endeavors to increase their country's war potential and opposed all bellicose and annexationist policies.

But the liberal policy of peace which, in the early sixties of the last century, as liberalism swept from one victory to another, was considered as already assured, at least in Europe, was based on the assumption that the people of every territory would have the right to determine for themselves the state to which they wished to belong. However, in order to secure this right, since the absolutist powers had no intention of peacefully relinquishing their prerogatives, a number of rather serious wars and revolutions were first necessary. The overthrow of foreign domination in Italy, the preservation of the Germans in Schleswig-Holstein in the face of threatening denationalization, the liberation of the Poles and of the South Slavs could be attempted only by force of arms. In only one of the many places where the existing political order found itself opposed by a demand for the right of self-determination could the issue be peacefully resolved: liberal England freed the Ionian islands. Everywhere else the same situation resulted in wars and revolutions. From the struggles to form a unified German state developed the disastrous modern Franco-German conflict; the Polish question remained unresolved because the Czar crushed one rebellion after another; the Balkan question was only partially settled; and the impossibility of solving the problems of the Hapsburg monarchy against the will of the ruling dynasty ultimately led to the incident that became the immediate cause of the World War.

Modern imperialism is distinguished from the expansionist tendencies of the absolute principalities by the fact that its moving spirits are not the members of the ruling dynasty, nor even of the nobility, the bureaucracy, or the officers' corps of the army bent on personal enrichment and aggrandizement by plundering the resources of conquered territories, but the mass of the people, who look upon it as the most appropriate means for the preservation of national independence. In the complex network of antiliberal policies, which have so far expanded the functions of the state as to leave hardly any field of human activity free of government interference, it is futile to hope for even a moderately satisfactory solution of the political problems of the areas in which members of several nationalities live side by side. If the government of these territories is not conducted along completely liberal lines, there can be no question of even an approach to equality of rights in the treatment of the various national groups. There can then be only rulers and those ruled. The only choice is whether one will be hammer or anvil. Thus, the striving for as strong a national state as possible—one that can extend its control to all territories of mixed nationality—becomes an indispensable requirement of national self-preservation.

But the problem of linguistically mixed areas is not limited to countries long settled. Capitalism opens up for civilization new lands offering more favorable conditions of production than great parts of the countries that have been long inhabited. Capital and labor flow to the most favorable location. The migratory movement thus initiated exceeds by far all the previous migrations of the peoples of the world. Only a few nations can have their emigrants move to lands in which political power is in the hands of their compatriots. Where, however, this condition does not prevail, the migration gives rise once again to all those conflicts that generally develop in polyglot territories. In particular cases, into which we shall not enter here, matters are somewhat different in the areas of overseas colonization than in the long-settled countries of Europe. Nevertheless, the conflicts that spring from the unsatisfactory situation of national minorities are, in the last analysis, identical. The desire of each country to preserve its own nationals from such a fate leads, on the one hand, to the struggle for the acquisition of colonies suitable for settlement by Europeans, and, on the other hand, to the adoption of the policy of using import duties to protect domestic production operating under less favorable conditions against the superior competition of foreign industry, in the hope of thereby making the emigration of workers unnecessary. Indeed, in order to expand the protected market as far as possible, efforts are made to acquire even territories that are not regarded as suitable for European settlement. We may date the beginning of modern imperialism from the late seventies of the last century, when the industrial countries of Europe started to abandon the policy of free trade and to engage in the race for colonial "markets" in Africa and Asia.

It was in reference to England that the term "imperialism" was first employed to characterize the modern policy of territorial expansion. England's imperialism, to be sure, was primarily directed, not so much toward the incorporation of new territories as toward the creation of an area of uniform commercial policy out of the various possessions subject to the King of England. This was the result of the peculiar situation in which England found itself as the mother country of the most extensive colonial settlements in the world. Nevertheless, the end that the English imperialists sought to attain in the creation of a customs union embracing the dominions and the mother country was the same as that which the colonial acquisitions of Germany, Italy, France, Belgium, and other European countries were intended to serve, viz., the creation of protected export markets.

The grand commercial objectives aimed at by the policy of imperialism were nowhere attained. The dream of an all-British customs union remained unrealized. The territories annexed by European countries in the last decades, as well as those in which they were able to obtain "concessions," play such a subordinate role in the provision of raw materials and half-manufactured goods for the world market and in their corresponding consumption of industrial products that no essential change in conditions could be brought about by such arrangements. In order to attain the goals that imperialism aimed at, it was not enough for the nations of Europe to occupy areas inhabited by savages incapable of resistance. They had to reach out for territories that were in the possession of peoples ready and able to defend themselves. And it is here that the policy of imperialism suffered shipwreck, or will soon do so. In Abyssinia, in Mexico, in the Caucasus, in Persia, in China—everywhere we see the imperialist aggressors in retreat or at least already in great difficulties.

## 6. Colonial Policy

The considerations and objectives that have guided the colonial policy of the European powers since the age of the great discoveries stand in the sharpest contrast to all the principles of liberalism. The basic idea of colonial policy was to take advantage of the military superiority of the white race over the members of other races. The Europeans set out, equipped with all the weapons and contrivances that their civilization placed at their disposal, to subjugate weaker peoples, to rob them of their property, and to enslave them. Attempts have been made to extenuate and gloss over the true motive of colonial policy with the excuse that its sole object was to make it possible for primitive peoples to share in the blessings of European civilization. Even assuming that this was the real objective of the governments that sent out conquerors to distant parts of the world, the liberal could still not see any adequate basis for regarding this kind of colonization as useful or beneficial. If, as we believe, European civilization really is superior to that of the primitive tribes of Africa or to the civilizations of Asia—estimable though the latter may be in their own way—it should be able to prove its superiority by inspiring these peoples to adopt it of their own accord. Could there be a more doleful proof of the sterility of European civilization than that it can be spread by no other means than fire and sword?

No chapter of history is steeped further in blood than the history of colonialism. Blood was shed uselessly and senselessly. Flourishing lands were laid waste; whole peoples destroyed and exterminated. All this can in no way be extenuated or justified. The dominion of Europeans in Africa and in important parts of Asia is absolute. It stands in the sharpest contrast to all the principles of liberalism and democracy, and there can be no doubt that we must strive for its abolition. The only question is how the elimination of this intolerable condition can be accomplished in the least harmful way possible.

The most simple and radical solution would be for the European governments to withdraw their officials, soldiers, and police from these areas and to leave the inhabitants to themselves. It is of no consequence whether this is done immediately or whether a freely held plebiscite of the natives is made to precede the surrender of the colonies. For there can scarcely be any doubt as to the outcome of a truly free election. European rule in the overseas colonies cannot count on the consent of its subjects.

The immediate consequence of this radical solution would be, if not outright anarchy, then at least continual conflicts in the areas evacuated by the Europeans. It may be safely taken for granted that up to now the natives have learned only evil ways from the Europeans, and not good ones. This is not the fault of the natives, but rather of their European conquerors, who have taught them nothing but evil. They have brought arms and engines of destruction of all kinds to the colonies; they have sent out their worst and most brutal individuals as officials and officers; at the point of the sword they have set up a colonial rule that in its sanguinary cruelty rivals the despotic system of the Bolsheviks. Europeans must not be surprised if the bad example that they themselves have set in their colonies now bears evil fruit. In any case, they have no right to complain pharisaically about the low state of public morals among the natives. Nor would they be justified in maintaining that the natives are not yet mature enough for freedom and that they still need at least several years of further education under the lash of foreign rulers before they are capable of being left on their own. For this "education" itself is at least partly responsible for the terrible conditions that exist today in the colonies, even though its consequences will not make themselves fully apparent until after the eventual withdrawal of European troops and officials.

But perhaps it will be contended that it is the duty of the Europeans, as members of a superior race, to avoid the anarchy that would presumably break out after the evacuation of the colonies and therefore to maintain their dominion in the interests and for the benefit of the natives themselves. In order to strengthen this argument, a lurid picture may be painted of the conditions that existed in Central Africa and in many parts of Asia before the establishment of European rule. One may recall the hunts for slaves conducted by the Arabs in Central Africa and the wanton outrages that many Indian despots allowed themselves. Of course, there is much that is hypocritical in this mode of argumentation, and one should not forget, for example, that the slave trade in Africa could prosper only because the descendants of Europeans in the American colonies entered the slave market as buyers. But it is not at all necessary for us to go into the pros and cons of this line of reasoning. If all that can be adduced in favor of the maintenance of European rule in the colonies is the supposed interest of the natives, then one must say that it would be better if this rule were brought to an end completely. No one has a right to thrust himself into the affairs of others in order to further their interest, and no one ought, when he has his own interests in view, to pretend that he is acting selflessly only in the interest of others.

There is, however, yet another argument in favor of the continuance of European authority and influence in the colonial areas. If the Europeans had never brought the tropical colonies under their dominion, if they had not made their economic system dependent to a considerable extent on the importation of tropical raw materials and overseas agricultural products that they paid for with industrial goods, it would still be possible to discuss quite calmly the question whether or not it is advisable to draw these areas into the network of the world market. But since colonization has already forced all these territories into the framework of the world-wide economic community, the situation is quite different. The economy of Europe today is based, to a great extent, on the inclusion of Africa and large parts of Asia in the world economy as suppliers of raw materials of all kinds. These raw materials are not taken from the natives of these areas by force. They are not carried away as tribute, but handed over in voluntary exchange for the industrial products of Europe. Thus, relations are not founded on any one-sided advantage; they are, on the contrary, mutually beneficial, and the inhabitants of the colonies derive from them just as many advantages as the inhabitants of England or Switzerland. Any stoppage in these trade relations would involve serious economic losses for Europe as well as for the colonies and would sharply depress the standard of living of great masses of people. If the slow extension of economic relations over the whole earth and the gradual development of the world economy was one of the most important sources of the increasing wealth of the last hundred and fifty years, a reversal of this trend would represent for the world an economic catastrophe of hitherto unprecedented proportions. In its extent and consequences, this catastrophe would exceed by far the crisis connected with the economic consequences of the World War. Ought the well-being of Europe and, at the same time, that of the colonies as well to be allowed to decline further in order to give the natives a chance to determine their own political destinies, when this would lead, in any event, not to their freedom, but merely to a change of masters?

This is the consideration that must be decisive in judging questions of colonial policy. European officials, troops, and police must remain in these areas, as far as their presence is necessary in order to maintain the legal and political conditions required to insure the participation of the colonial territories in international trade. It must be possible to carry on commercial, industrial, and agricultural operations in the colonies, to exploit mines, and to bring the products of the country, by rail and river, to the coast and thence to Europe and America. That all this should continue to be possible is in the interest of everyone, not only of the inhabitants of Europe, America, and Australia, but also of the natives of Asia and Africa themselves. Wherever the colonial powers do not go beyond this in the treatment of their colonies, one can raise no objection to their activities even from the liberal standpoint.

But everyone knows how seriously all the colonial powers have sinned against this principle. It is hardly necessary to recall the horrors that trustworthy English correspondents have reported as having been perpetrated in the Belgian Congo. Let us assume that these atrocities were not intended by the Belgian government and are only to be attributed to the excesses and evil characters of the functionaries sent out to the Congo. Yet the very fact that almost all the colonial powers have established in their overseas possessions a commercial system that grants a favored position to the goods of the mother country shows that present-day colonial policy is dominated by considerations altogether different from those that ought to prevail in this field.

In order to bring the interests of Europe and of the white race into harmony with those of the colored races in the colonies in regard to all questions of economic policy, the League of Nations must be given supreme authority in the administration of all those overseas territories in which there is no system of parliamentary government. The League would have to see to it that self-government is granted as soon as possible to the lands that today do not yet possess it and that the authority of the mother country is limited to the protection of property, of the civil rights of foreigners, and of trade relations. The natives as well as the nationals of other powers must be granted the right to bring complaints directly to the League if any measures of the mother country exceed what is required to guarantee the security of trade and commerce and of economic activity in general in these territories, and the League of Nations must be granted the right to make an effective settlement of such complaints.

The application of these principles would mean, in effect, that all the overseas territories of the European countries would at first be turned into mandates of the League. But even this would have to be viewed only as a transitional stage. The final goal must continue to be the complete liberation of the colonies from the despotic rule under which they live today.

With this solution to a difficult problem—which is becoming ever more difficult with the passage of time—not only the nations of Europe and America that do not possess colonies, but also the colonial powers and the natives would have to be content. The colonial powers have to realize that in the long run they will not be able to maintain their dominion over the colonies. As capitalism has penetrated into these territories, the natives have become self-reliant; there is no longer any cultural disparity between their upper classes and the officers and officials who are in charge of the administration on behalf of the mother country. Militarily and politically, the distribution of power today is quite different from what it was even a generation ago. The attempt of the European powers, the United States, and Japan to treat

China as a colonial territory has proved a failure. In Egypt, the English are even now in retreat; in India, they are already in a defensive position. That the Netherlands would be unable to hold the East Indies against a really serious attack is well known. The same is true of the French colonies in Africa and Asia. The Americans are not happy with the Philippines and would be prepared to give them up if a suitable occasion presented itself. The transfer of the colonies to the care of the League of Nations would guarantee to the colonial powers the undiminished possession of their capital investments and protect them against having to make sacrifices to quell native uprisings. The natives too could only be grateful for a proposal that would assure them independence by way of a peaceful evolution and with it the guarantee that no neighbor bent on conquest would threaten their political independence in the future.

### 7. *Free Trade*

The theoretical demonstration of the consequences of the protective tariff and of free trade is the keystone of classical economics. It is so clear, so obvious, so indisputable, that its opponents were unable to advance any arguments against it that could not be immediately refuted as completely mistaken and absurd.

Nevertheless, nowadays we find protective tariffs—indeed, often even outright prohibitions on imports—all over the world. Even in England, the mother country of free trade, protectionism is in the ascendancy today. The principle of national autarky wins new supporters with every day that passes. Even countries with only a few million inhabitants, like Hungary and Czechoslovakia, are attempting, by means of a high-tariff policy and prohibitions on imports, to make themselves independent of the rest of the world. The basic idea of the foreign trade policy of the United States is to impose on all goods produced abroad at lower costs import duties to the full amount of this difference. What renders the whole situation grotesque is the fact that all countries want to decrease their imports, but at the same time to increase their exports. The effect of these policies is to interfere with the international division of labor and thereby generally to lower the productivity of labor. The only reason this result has not become more noticeable is that the advances of the capitalist system have always been so far sufficient to outweigh it. However, there can be no doubt that everyone today would be richer if the protective tariff did not artificially drive production from more favorable to less favorable localities.

Under a system of completely free trade, capital and labor would be employed wherever conditions are most favorable for production. Other locations would be used as long as it was still possible to produce anywhere under more favorable conditions. To the extent to which, as a result of the development of the means of transportation, improvements in technology, and more thorough exploration of countries newly opened to commerce, it is discovered that there are sites more favorable for production than those currently being used, production shifts to these localities. Capital and labor tend to move from areas where conditions are less favorable for production to those in which they are more favorable.

But the migration of capital and labor presupposes not only complete freedom of trade, but also the complete absence of obstacles to their movement from one country to another. This was far from being the case at the time that the classical free-trade doctrine was first developed. A whole series of obstacles stood in the way of the free movement of both capital and labor. Because of ignorance of conditions, a general insecurity in regard to law and order, and a number of similar reasons, capitalists felt reluctant about investing in foreign countries. As for the workers, they found it impossible to leave their native land, not only because of their ignorance of foreign languages, but because of legal, religious, and other difficulties. At the beginning of the nineteenth century, it was, to be sure, generally true that capital and labor could move freely within each country, but obstacles stood in the way of their movement from one country to another. The sole justification for distinguishing in economic theory between domestic and foreign trade is to be found in the fact that in the case of the former there is free mobility of capital and labor, whereas this is not true in regard to the commerce between nations. Thus, the problem that the classical theory had to solve may be stated as follows: What are the effects of free trade in consumers' goods between one country and another if the mobility of capital and labor from one to the other is restricted?

To this question Ricardo's doctrine provided the answer. The branches of production distribute themselves among the individual countries in such a way that each country devotes its resources to those industries in which it possesses the greatest superiority over other countries. The mercantilists had feared that a country with unfavorable conditions for production would import more than it would export, so that it would ultimately find itself without any money; and they demanded that protective tariffs and prohibitions on imports be decreed in time to prevent such a deplorable situation from arising. The classical doctrine shows that these mercantilist fears were groundless. For even a country in which the conditions of production in every branch of industry are less favorable than they are in other countries need not fear that it will export less than it will import. The classical doctrine demonstrated, in a brilliant and incontrovertible way that has never been contested by anybody, that even countries with relatively favorable conditions of production must find it advantageous to import from countries with comparatively unfavorable conditions of production those commodities that they would, to be sure, be better fitted to produce, but not so much better fitted as they are to produce other commodities in whose production they then specialize.

Thus, what the classical theory of free trade says to the statesman is: There are countries with relatively favorable and others with relatively unfavorable natural conditions of production. In the absence of interference on the part of governments, the international division of labor will, of itself, result in every country's finding its place in the world economy, no matter how its conditions of production compare with those of other countries. Of course, the countries with comparatively favorable conditions of production will be richer than the others, but this is a fact that cannot be altered by political measures in any case. It is simply the consequence of a difference in the natural factors of production.

This was the situation that confronted the older liberalism, and to this situation it responded with the classical doctrine of free trade. But since the days of Ricardo world conditions have changed considerably, and the problem that the free-trade doctrine had to face in the last sixty years before the outbreak of the World War was completely different from the one with which it had to deal at the close of the eighteenth and the beginning of the nineteenth century. For the nineteenth century partially eliminated the obstacles that, at its beginning, had stood in the way of the free mobility of capital and labor. In the second half of the nineteenth century it was far easier for a capitalist to invest his capital abroad than it had been in Ricardo's day. Law and order were established on a considerably firmer foundation; knowledge of foreign countries, manners, and customs had spread; and the joint-stock company offered the possibility of dividing the risk of foreign enterprises among many persons and thereby reducing it. It would, of course, be an exaggeration to say that at the beginning of the twentieth century capital was as mobile in its passage from one country to another as it was within the territory of the country itself. Certain differences still existed, to be sure; yet the assumption that capital had to remain within the boundaries of each country was no longer valid. Nor was this any longer true of labor either. In the second half of the nineteenth century millions left Europe to find better opportunities for employment overseas.

In so far as the conditions presupposed by the classical doctrine of free trade, viz., the immobility of capital and labor, no longer existed, the distinction between the effects of free trade in domestic commerce and in foreign commerce likewise necessarily lost its validity. If capital and labor can move as freely between one country and another as they do within the confines of each, then there is no further justification for making a distinction between the effects of free trade in domestic commerce and in foreign commerce. For then what was said in regard to the former holds for the latter as well: the result of free trade is that only those locations are used for production in which the conditions for it are comparatively favorable, while those in which the conditions of production are comparatively unfavorable remain unused. Capital and labor flow from the countries with less favorable conditions of production toward those where the conditions of production are more favorable, or, more precisely, from the long-settled, thickly populated European countries toward America and Australia, as areas that offer more favorable conditions of production.

For the European nations that had at their disposal, besides the old areas of settlement in Europe, overseas territories suitable for colonization by Europeans, this meant nothing more than that they now settled a part of their population overseas. In England's case, for example, some of her sons now lived in Canada, Australia, or South Africa. The emigrants who had left England could retain their English citizenship and nationality in their new homes. But for Germany the case was quite different. The German who emigrated landed in the territory of a foreign country and found himself among the members of a foreign nation. He became the citizen of a foreign state, and it was to be expected that after one, two, or at the most three generations, his attachment to the German people would be dissolved and the process of his assimilation as a member of a foreign nation would be completed. Germany was faced with the problem of whether it was to look on with indifference while a part of her capital and her people emigrated overseas.

One must not fall into the error of assuming that the problems of commercial policy that England and Germany had to face in the second half of the nineteenth century were the same. For England, it was a question of whether or not she ought to permit a number of her sons to emigrate to the dominions, and there was no reason to hinder their emigration in any way. For Germany, however, the problem was whether it ought to stand by quietly while her nationals emigrated to the British colonies, to South America, and to other countries, where it was to be expected that these emigrants, in the course of time, would give up their citizenship and nationality just as hundreds of thousands, indeed, millions, who had previously emigrated, had already done. Because it did not want this to happen, the German Empire, which during the sixties and seventies had been approaching ever more closely to a policy of free trade, now shifted, toward the end of the seventies, to one of protectionism by the imposition of import duties designed to shield German agriculture and industry against foreign competition. Under the protection of these tariffs German agriculture was able to some extent to bear East-European and overseas competition from farms operating on better land, and German industry could form cartels that kept the domestic price above the price on the world market, enabling it to use the profits thereby realized to undersell its competitors abroad.

But the ultimate goal that was aimed at in the return to protectionism could not be achieved. The higher living and production costs rose in Germany as a direct consequence of these protective tariffs, the more difficult its trade position necessarily became. To be sure, it was possible for Germany to make a mighty industrial upswing in the first three decades of the era of the new commercial policy. But this upswing would have occurred even in the absence of a protective tariff, for it was primarily the result of the introduction of new methods in the German iron and chemical industries, which enabled them to make better use of the country's abundant natural resources.

Antiliberal policy, by abolishing the free mobility of labor in international trade and considerably restricting even the mobility of capital, has, to a certain extent, eliminated the difference that existed in the conditions of international trade between the beginning and the end of the nineteenth century and has reverted to those prevailing at the time the doctrine of free trade was first formulated. Once again capital and, above all, labor are hindered in their movements. Under the conditions existing today, unhampered trade in consumers' goods could not give rise to any migratory movements. Once again, it would result in a state of affairs in which the individual peoples of the world would be engaged in those types and branches of production

136 Liberalism: A Socio-Economic Exposition

for which the relatively best conditions exist in their own countries.

But whatever may be the prerequisites for the development of international trade, protective tariffs can accomplish only *one* thing: to prevent production from being carried on where the natural and social conditions are most favorable for it and to cause it to be carried on instead where conditions are worse. The outcome of protectionism is, therefore, always a reduction in the productivity of human labor. The freetrader is far from denying that the evil that the nations of the world wish to combat by means of a policy of protectionism really is an evil. What he maintains is only that the means recommended by the imperialists and protectionists cannot eliminate that evil. He therefore proposes a different way. In order to create the indispensable conditions for a lasting peace, one of the features of the present international situation that the liberal wishes to change is the fact that emigrants from nations like Germany and Italy, which have been treated like stepchildren in the division of the world, must live in areas in which, because of the adoption of antiliberal policies, they are condemned to lose their nationality.

## 8. *Freedom of Movement*

Liberalism has sometimes been reproached on the ground that its program is predominantly negative. This follows necessarily, it is asserted, from the very nature of freedom, which can be conceived only as freedom *from* something, for the demand for freedom consists essentially in the rejection of some sort of claim. On the other hand, it is thought, the program of the authoritarian parties is positive. Since a very definite value judgment is generally connoted by the terms "negative" and "positive," this way of speaking already involves a surreptitious attempt to discredit the political program of liberalism.

There is no need to repeat here once again that the liberal program—a society based on private ownership of the means of production—is no less positive than any other conceivable political program. What is negative in the liberal program is the denial, the rejection, and the combatting of everything that stands in opposition to this positive program. In this defensive posture, the program of liberalism—and, for that matter, that of every movement—is dependent on the position that its opponents assume towards it. Where the opposition is strongest, the assault of liberalism must also be strongest; where it is relatively weak or even completely lacking, a few brief words, under the circumstances, are sufficient. And since the opposition that liberalism has had to confront has changed during the course of history, the defensive aspect of the liberal program has also undergone many changes.

This becomes most clearly evident in the stand that it takes in regard to the question of freedom of movement. The liberal demands that every person have the right to live wherever he wants. This is not a "negative" demand. It belongs to the very essence of a society based on private ownership of the means of production that every man may work and dispose of his earnings where he thinks best. This principle takes on a negative character only if it encounters forces aiming at a restriction of freedom of movement. In this negative aspect, the right to freedom of movement has, in the course of time, undergone a complete change. When liberalism arose in the eighteenth and nineteenth centuries, it had to struggle for freedom of emigration. Today, the struggle is over freedom of immigration. At that time, it had to oppose laws which hindered the inhabitants of a country from moving to the city and which held out the prospect of severe punishment for anyone who wanted to leave his native land in order to better himself in a foreign land. Immigration, however, was at that time generally free and unhampered.

Today, as is well known, things are quite different. The trend began some decades ago with laws against the immigration of Chinese coolies. Today in every country in the world that could appear inviting to immigration, there are more or less stringent laws either prohibiting it entirely or at least restricting it severely.

This policy must be considered from two points of view: first, as a policy of the trade unions, and then as a policy of national protectionism.

Aside from such coercive measures as the closed shop, compulsory strikes, and violent interference with those willing to work, the only way the trade unions can have any influence on the labor market is by restricting the supply of labor. But since it is not within the power of the trade unions to reduce the number of workers living in the world, the only other possibility remaining open to them is to block access to employment, and thus diminish the number of workers, in one branch of industry or in one country at the expense of the workers employed in other industries or living in other countries. For reasons of practical politics, it is possible only to a limited extent for those engaged in a particular branch of industry to bar from it the rest of the workers in the country. On the other hand, no special political difficulty is involved in imposing such restrictions on the entrance of foreign labor.

The natural conditions of production and, concomitantly, the productivity of labor are more favorable, and, as a consequence, wage rates are higher, in the United States than in vast areas of Europe. In the absence of immigration barriers, European workers would emigrate to the United States in great numbers to look for jobs. The American immigration laws make this exceptionally difficult. Thus, the wages of labor in the United States are kept above the height that they would reach if there were full freedom of migration, whereas in Europe they are depressed below this height. On the one hand, the American worker gains; on the other hand, the European worker loses.

However, it would be a mistake to consider the consequences of immigration barriers exclusively from the point of view of their immediate effect on wages. They go further. As a result of the relative oversupply of labor in areas with comparatively unfavorable conditions of production, and the relative shortage of labor in areas in which the conditions of production are comparatively favorable, production is further expanded in the former and more restricted in the latter than would be the case if there were full freedom of migration. Thus, the effects of restricting this freedom are just the same as those of a protective tariff. In one part of the world comparatively favorable opportunities for production are not utilized, while in another part of the world less favorable opportunities for production are being exploited. Looked at from the standpoint of humanity, the result is a lowering of the productivity of human labor, a reduction in the supply of goods at the disposal of mankind.

Attempts to justify on economic grounds the policy of restricting immigration are therefore doomed from the outset. There cannot be the slightest doubt that migration barriers diminish the productivity of human labor. When the trade unions of the United States or Australia hinder immigration, they are fighting not only against the interests of the workers of the rest of the countries of the world, but also against the interests of everyone else in order to secure a special privilege for themselves. For all that, it still remains quite uncertain whether the increase in the general productivity of human labor which could be brought about by the establishment of complete freedom of migration would not be so great as to compensate entirely the members of the American and Australian trade unions for the losses that they could suffer from the immigration of foreign workers.

The workers of the United States and Australia could not succeed in having restrictions imposed on immigration if they did not have still another argument to fall back upon in support of their policy. After all, even today the power of certain liberal principles and ideas is so great that one cannot combat them if one does not place allegedly higher and more important considerations above the interest in the attainment of maximum productivity. We have already seen how "national interests" are cited in justification of protective tariffs. The same considerations are also invoked in favor of restrictions on immigration.

In the absence of any migration barriers whatsoever, vast hordes of immigrants from the comparatively overpopulated areas of Europe would, it is maintained, inundate Australia and America. They would come in such great numbers that it would no longer be possible to count on their assimilation. If in the past immigrants to America soon adopted the English language and American ways and customs, this was in part due to the fact that they did not come over all at once in such great numbers. The small groups of immigrants who distributed themselves over a wide land quickly integrated themselves into the great body of the American people. The individual immigrant was already half assimilated when the next immigrants landed on American soil. One of the most important reasons for this rapid national assimilation was the fact that the immigrants from foreign countries did not come in too great numbers. This, it is believed, would now change, and there is real danger that the ascendancy— or more correctly, the exclusive dominion—of the Anglo-Saxons in the United States would be destroyed. This is especially to be feared in the case of heavy immigration on the part of the Mongolian peoples of Asia.

These fears may perhaps be exaggerated in regard to the United States. As regards Australia, they certainly are not. Australia has approximately the same number of inhabitants as Austria; its area, however, is a hundred times greater than Austria's, and its natural resources are certainly incomparably richer. If Australia were thrown open to immigration, it can be assumed with great probability that its population would in a few years consist mostly of Japanese, Chinese, and Malayans.

The aversion that most people feel today towards the members of foreign nationalities and especially towards those of other races is evidently too great to admit of any peaceful settlement of such antagonisms. It is scarcely to be expected that the Australians will voluntarily permit the immigration of Europeans not of English nationality, and it is completely out of the question that they should permit Asiatics too to seek work and a permanent home in their continent. The Australians of English descent insist that the fact that it was the English who first opened up this land for settlement has given the English people a special right to the exclusive possession of the entire continent for all time to come. The members of the world's other nationalities, however, do not in the least desire to contest the right of the Australians to occupy any of the land that they already are making use of in Australia. They think only that it is unfair that the Australians do not permit the utilization of more favorable conditions of production that today lie fallow and force them to carry on production under the less favorable conditions prevailing in their own countries.

This issue is of the most momentous significance for the future of the world. Indeed, the fate of civilization depends on its satisfactory resolution. On the one side stand scores, indeed, hundreds of millions of Europeans and Asiatics who are compelled to work under less favorable conditions of production than they could find in the territories from which they are barred. They demand that the gates of the forbidden paradise be opened to them so that they may increase the productivity of their labor and thereby receive for themselves a higher standard of living. On the other side stand those already fortunate enough to call their own the land with the more favorable conditions of production. They desire—as far as they are workers, and not owners of the means of production—not to give up the higher wages that this position guarantees them. The entire nation, however, is unanimous in fearing inundation by foreigners. The present inhabitants of these favored lands fear that some day they could be reduced to a minority in their own country and that they would then have to suffer all the horrors of national persecution to which, for instance, the Germans are today exposed in Czechoslovakia, Italy, and Poland.

It cannot be denied that these fears are justified. Because of the enormous power that today stands at the command of the state, a national minority must expect the worst from a majority of a different nationality. As long as the state is granted the vast powers which it has today and which public opinion considers to be its right, the thought of having to live in a state whose government is in the hands of members of a foreign nationality is positively terrifying. It is frightful to live in a state in which at every turn one is exposed to persecution—masquerading under the guise of justice—by a ruling majority. It is dreadful to be handicapped even as a child in school on account of one's nationality and to be in the wrong before every judicial and administrative authority because one belongs to a national minority.

If one considers the conflict from this point of view, it seems as if it allows of no other solution than war. In that case, it is to be expected that the nation inferior in numbers will be defeated, that, for example, the nations of Asia, counting hundreds of millions, will succeed in driving the progeny of the white race from Australia. But we do not wish to indulge in such conjectures. For it is certain that such wars—and we must assume that a world problem of such great dimensions cannot be solved once and for all in just *one* war—would lead to the most frightful catastrophe for civilization.

It is clear that no solution of the problem of immigration is possible if one adheres to the ideal of the interventionist state, which meddles in every field of human activity, or to that of the socialist state. Only the adoption of the liberal program could make the problem of immigration, which today seems insoluble, completely disappear. In an Australia governed according to liberal principles, what difficulties could arise from the fact that in some parts of the continent Japanese and in other parts Englishmen were in the majority?

## 9. *The United States of Europe*

The United States of America is the mightiest and richest nation in the world. Nowhere else was capitalism able to develop more freely and with less interference from the government. The inhabitants of the United States of America are therefore far richer than those of any other country on earth. For more than sixty years their country was not involved in any war. If they had not waged a war of extermination against the original inhabitants of the land, if they had not needlessly waged war against Spain in 1898, and if they had not participated in the World War, only a few graybeards among them would today be able to give a first-hand account of what war means. It is doubtful whether the Americans themselves appreciate how much they owe to the fact that more of the policies of liberalism and capitalism have been realized in their country than in any other. Even foreigners do not know what it is that has made the much-envied republic rich and powerful. But—apart from those who, filled with resentment, affect a profound contempt for the "materialism" of American culture—all are agreed in desiring nothing more eagerly than that their country should be as rich and as powerful as the United States.

In various quarters it is being proposed, as the simplest way to achieve this end, that a "United States of Europe" be formed. By themselves the individual countries of the European continent are too thinly populated and do not have enough land at their disposal to be able to hold their own in the international struggle for supremacy as against the ever increasing power of the United States, against Russia, against the British Empire, against China, and against other groupings of similar size that may be formed in the future, perhaps in South America. They must therefore consolidate into a military and political union, into a defensive and offensive alliance, which alone would be capable of assuring to Europe in the centuries to come the importance in world politics that it has enjoyed in the past. What gives special support to the idea of a Pan-European union is the realization, which is every day impressing itself more strongly on everyone, that nothing can be more absurd than the protective tariff policies presently being pursued by the nations of Europe. Only the further development of the international division of labor can increase the well-being and produce the abundance of goods needed to raise the standard of living, and thereby also the cultural level, of the masses. The economic policies of all countries, but especially those of the smaller European nations, are aimed precisely at destroying the international division of labor. If the conditions under which American industry operates, with a potential market of more than a hundred twenty million rich consumers, unhampered by tariffs or similar obstacles, are compared with those against which German, Czechoslovakian, or Hungarian industry must contend, the utter absurdity of endeavors to create little autarkic economic territories becomes immediately obvious.

The evils that those who champion the idea of a United States of Europe are trying to combat undoubtedly exist, and the sooner they are eliminated, the better. But the formation of a United

States of Europe would not be an appropriate means to achieve this end.

Any reform in international relations must aim at abolishing a situation in which each country seeks in every way possible to enlarge its territory at the expense of other countries. The problem of international boundaries, which has assumed such overwhelming importance today, must lose all its significance. The nations must come to realize that the most important problem of foreign policy is the establishment of lasting peace, and they must understand that this can be assured throughout the world only if the field of activity permitted to the state is limited to the narrowest range. Only then will the size and extent of the territory subject to the sovereignty of the state no longer assume such overwhelming importance for the life of the individual as to make it seem natural, now as in the past, for rivers of blood to be shed in disputes over boundaries. The narrow-mindedness which sees nothing beyond one's own state and one's own nation and which has no conception of the importance of international cooperation must be replaced by a cosmopolitan outlook. This, however, is possible only if the society of nations, the international superstate, is so constituted that no people and no individual is oppressed on account of nationality or national peculiarities.

Nationalist policies, which always begin by aiming at the ruination of one's neighbor, must, in the final analysis, lead to the ruination of all. In order to overcome such provincialism and to replace it by a policy genuinely cosmopolitan in its orientation, it is first necessary for the nations of the world to realize that their interests do not stand in mutual opposition and that every nation best serves its own cause when it is intent on promoting the development of all nations and scrupulously abstains from every attempt to use violence against other nations or parts of other nations. Thus, what is needed is not the replacement of national chauvinism by a chauvinism that would have some larger, supranational entity for its object, but rather the recognition that every sort of chauvinism is mistaken. The old, militaristic methods of international politics must now give way to new, peaceful methods aiming at cooperative effort, and not at mutual warfare.

The champions of Pan-Europe and of the United States of Europe, however, have other ends in view. They do not plan on establishing a new kind of state different in its policies from the imperialistic and militaristic states that have existed up to now, but on a reconstitution of the old imperialistic and militaristic idea of the state. Pan-Europe is to be greater than the individual states that will comprise it; it is to be more powerful than they are and therefore more efficient militarily and better suited to oppose such great powers as England, the United States of America, and Russia. A European chauvinism is to take the place of the French, the German, or the Hungarian variety; a united front formed of all the European nations is to be directed against "foreigners": Britons, Americans, Russians, Chinese, and Japanese.

Now one can base a chauvinistic political consciousness and a chauvinistic military policy on a national foundation, but not on a geographic one. Community of language binds members of the same nationality close together, while linguistic diversity gives rise to a gulf between nations. If it were not for this fact—aside from all ideologies—chauvinistic thinking would never have been able to develop. The geographer, with map in hand, may, no doubt, very well view the European continent (with the exception of Russia) as a unity if he is so minded; but this does not create among the inhabitants of that region any feeling of community or solidarity on which the statesman could base his plans. A Rhinelander can be made to understand that he is defending his own cause if he goes into battle for the Germans of East Prussia. It may even be possible to bring him to see that the cause of all mankind is also his own cause. But he will never be able to understand that, while he has to stand side by side with the Portuguese because they too are Europeans, the cause of England is that of an enemy, or, at best, of a neutral alien. It is not possible to efface from men's minds (nor, incidentally, does liberalism have any desire to do so) the imprint left by a long historical development that has brought it about that the heart of a German beats faster at every mention of Germany, of the German people, or of all that is typically German. This feeling of nationality existed before any political attempt was made to base upon it the idea of a German state, a German policy, and German chauvinism. All the well-intentioned schemes for replacing national states by a federation of states, whether Central European, Pan-European, Pan-American, or constructed on some similar artificial basis, suffer from the same fundamental defect. They fail to take account of the fact that the words "Europe" or "Pan-Europe" and "European" or "Pan-European" do not have this kind of emotional connotation and are thus incapable of evoking sentiments of the kind called forth by such words as "Germany" and "German."

The matter may be seen in its clearest light if we direct our attention to the problem, which plays a decisive role in all these projects, of agreeing on a commercial policy for such a federation of states. As conditions are today, a Bavarian can be induced to regard the protection of German labor—let us say, in Saxony—as a sufficient justification for a tariff that makes it more expensive for him, the Bavarian, to purchase some article. We may hope that some day he will succeed in being converted to the realization that all political measures designed to achieve autarky, and hence all protective tariffs, are senseless and self-defeating and consequently ought to be abolished. But never will one succeed in inducing a Pole or a Hungarian to consider it justified that he should pay more than the world market price for any commodity merely in order to enable the French, the Germans, or the Italians to carry on its production in their countries. One can certainly win support for a policy of protectionism by combining an appeal to feelings of national solidarity with the nationalistic doctrine that the interests of different nations are mutually incompatible; but there is nothing similar that could serve a federation of states as an ideological basis for a system of protectionism. It is manifestly absurd to break up the ever increasing unity of world economy into a number of small national territories, each as autarkic as possible. But one cannot counteract the policy of economic isolation on a national scale by replacing it with the same policy on the part of a larger political entity comprising a number of different nationalities. The only way to counteract tendencies toward protectionism and autarky is to recognize their harmfulness and to appreciate the harmony of the interests of all nations.

Once it has been demonstrated that the disintegration of the world economy into a number of small autarkic areas has detrimental consequences for all nations, the conclusion in favor of free trade necessarily follows. In order to prove that a Pan-European zone of autarky should be set up under the shelter of a protective tariff, it would first be necessary to demonstrate that the interests of the Portuguese and the Rumanians, although in harmony with each other, both collide with those of Brazil and Russia. One would have to adduce proof that it is good for the Hungarians to give up their domestic textile industry in favor of the German, the French, and the Belgian, but that the interests of the Hungarians would be injured by the importation of English or American textiles.

The movement in favor of the formation of a federation of European states has arisen from a correct recognition of the untenability of all forms of chauvinistic nationalism. But what the supporters of this movement wish to set in its place is impracticable because it lacks a vital basis in the consciousness of the people. And even if the goal of the Pan-European movement could be achieved, the world would not be in the least the better for it. The struggle of a united European continent against the great world powers outside its territory would be no less ruinous than is the present struggle of the countries of Europe among themselves.

## 10. The League of Nations

Just as, in the eyes of the liberal, the state is not the highest ideal, so it is also not the best apparatus of compulsion. The metaphysical theory of the state declares—approaching, in this respect, the vanity and presumption of the absolute monarchs—that each individual state is sovereign, i.e., that it represents the last and highest court of appeals. But, for the liberal, the world does not end at the borders of the state. In his eyes, whatever significance national boundaries have is only incidental and subordinate. His political thinking encompasses the whole of mankind. The starting-point of his entire political philosophy is the conviction that the division of labor is international and not merely national. He realizes from the very first that it is not sufficient to establish peace within each country, that it is much more important that all nations live at peace with one another. The liberal therefore demands that the political organization of society be extended until it reaches its culmination in a world state that unites all nations on an equal basis. For this reason he sees the law of each nation as subordinate to international law, and that is why he demands supranational tribunals and administrative authorities to assure peace among nations in the same way that the judicial and executive organs of each country are charged with the maintenance of peace within its own territory.

For a long time the demand for the establishment of such a supranational world organization was confined to a few thinkers who were considered utopians and went unheeded. To be sure, after the end of the Napoleonic Wars, the world repeatedly witnessed the spectacle of the statesmen of the leading powers gathered around the conference table to arrive at a common accord, and after the middle of the nineteenth century, an increasing number of supranational institutions were established, the most widely noted of which are the Red Cross and the International Postal Union. Yet all of this was still a very far cry from the creation of a genuine supranational organization. Even the Hague Peace Conference signified hardly any progress in this respect. It was only the horrors of the World War that first made it possible to win widespread support for the idea of an organization of all nations that would be in a position to prevent future conflicts. With the end of the war, the victors took steps to create an association which they called "The League of Nations" and which is widely held throughout the world to be the nucleus of what could be a really effective future international organization.

In any case, there can be no doubt that what today goes under that name is in no way a realization of the liberal ideal of a supranational organization. In the first place, some of the most important and powerful nations of the world do not belong to the League at all. The United States, not to mention smaller nations, still stands outside. Besides, the covenant of the League of Nations suffers from the very outset from the fact that it distinguishes between two categories of member states: those that enjoy full rights and those that, having been on the losing side in the World War, are not fully qualified members. It is clear that such an inequality of status in the community of nations must bear within itself the seeds of war in the same way that every such division into castes does within a country. All these shortcomings have combined to weaken the League lamentably and to render it impotent in regard to all the substantive questions with which it has been confronted. One has only to think of its conduct in the conflict between Italy and Greece or in regard to the Mosul question, and especially in those cases in which the fate of oppressed minorities depended on its decision.

There are in all countries, but especially in England and Germany, groups that believe that in the interest of transforming this sham League of Nations into a real one—into a genuine supranational state—its present weaknesses and defects should be treated in the most indulgent possible way. Such opportunism never does any good, no matter what question is at issue. The League of Nations is—and this would certainly have to be conceded by everybody except the functionaries and the staff employed in its bureaus—an inadequate institution in no way corresponding to the demands that one is entitled to make of a world organization. This fact, far from being minimized or ignored, needs to be repeatedly and insistently emphasized so that attention is called to all the changes that would have to be made in order to transform this sham into a real League of Nations. Nothing has done greater harm to the idea of a supranational world organization than the intellectual confusion arising from the belief that the present League constitutes a complete or virtually complete realization of what every honest and sincere liberal must demand. It is impossible to build a real League of Nations, capable of assuring lasting peace, on the principle that the traditional, historically determined boundaries of each country are to be treated as inalterably fixed. The League of Nations retains the fundamental defect of all previous international law: in setting up procedural rules for adjudicating disputes between nations, it is not in the least interested in creating any other norms for their settlement than the preservation of the *status quo* and the enforcement of existing treaties. Under such circumstances, however, peace cannot be assured unless it be by reducing the whole world situation to a state of frozen immobility.

To be sure, the League does hold out, even though very cautiously and with many reservations, the prospect of some future boundary adjustments to do justice to the demands of some nations and parts of nations. It also promises—again very cautiously and qualifiedly—protection to national minorities. This permits us to hope that from these extremely inadequate beginnings a world superstate really deserving of the name may some day be able to develop that would be capable of assuring the nations the peace that they require. But this question will not be decided at Geneva in the sessions of the present League, and certainly not in the parliaments of the individual countries that comprise it. For the problem involved is not at all a matter of organization or of the technique of international government, but the greatest ideological question that mankind has ever faced. It is a question of whether we shall succeed in creating throughout the world a frame of mind without which all agreements for the preservation of peace and all the proceedings of courts of arbitration will remain, at the crucial moment, only worthless scraps of paper. This frame of mind can be nothing less than the unqualified, unconditional acceptance of liberalism. Liberal thinking must permeate all nations, liberal principles must pervade all political institutions, if the prerequisites of peace are to be created and the causes of war eliminated. As long as nations cling to protective tariffs, immigration barriers, compulsory education, interventionism, and etatism, new conflicts capable of breaking out at any time into open warfare will continually arise to plague mankind.

## 11. *Russia*

The law-abiding citizen by his labor serves both himself and his fellow man and thereby integrates himself peacefully into the social order. The robber, on the other hand, is intent, not on honest toil, but on the forcible appropriation of the fruits of others' labor. For thousands of years the world had to submit to the yoke of military conquerors and feudal lords who simply took for granted that the products of the industry of other men existed for them to consume. The evolution of mankind towards civilization and the strengthening of social bonds required, first of all, overcoming the intellectual and physical influence of the military and feudal castes that aspired to rule the world and the substitution of the ideal of the bourgeois for that of the hereditary lord. The supplanting of the militaristic ideal, which esteems only the warrior and despises honest labor, has not, by any means, even yet been completely achieved. In every nation there are still individuals whose minds are altogether taken up with the ideas and images of the militaristic ages. There are nations in which transient atavistic impulses toward plunder and violence, which one would have presumed to have long since been mastered, still break out and once more gain ascendancy. But, by and large, one can say of the nations of the white race that today inhabit central and western Europe and America that the mentality that Herbert Spencer called "militaristic" has been displaced by that to which he gave the name "industrial." Today there is only *one* great nation that steadfastly adheres to the militaristic ideal, viz., the Russians.

Of course, even among the Russian people there are some who do not share this attitude. It is only to be regretted that they have not been able to prevail over their compatriots. Ever since Russia was first in a position to exercise an influence on European politics, it has continually behaved like a robber who lies in wait for the moment when he can pounce upon his victim and plunder him of his possessions. At no time did the Russian Czars acknowledge any other limits to the expansion of their empire than those dictated by the force of circumstances. The position of the Bolsheviks in regard to the problem of the territorial expansion of their dominions is not a whit different. They too acknowledge no other rule than that, in the conquest of new lands, one may and indeed must go as far as one dares, with due regard to one's resources. The fortunate circumstance that saved civilization from being destroyed by the Russians was the fact that the nations of Europe were strong enough to be able successfully to stand off the onslaught of the hordes of Russian barbarians. The experiences of the Russians in the Napoleonic Wars, the Crimean War, and the Turkish campaign of 1877-78 showed them that, in spite of the great number of their soldiers, their army is unable to seize the offensive against Europe. The World War merely confirmed this.

More dangerous than bayonets and cannon are the weapons of the mind. To be sure, the response that the ideas of the Russians found in Europe was due, in the first place, to the fact that Europe itself was already full of these ideas before they came out of Russia. Indeed, it would perhaps be more nearly correct to say that these Russian ideas themselves were not originally Russian, however much they may have suited the character of the Russian people, but that they were borrowed by the Russians from Europe. So great is the intellectual sterility of the Russians that they were never able to formulate for themselves the expression of their own inmost nature.

Liberalism, which is based completely on science and whose policies represent nothing but the application of the results of science, must be on its guard not to make unscientific value judgments. Value judgments stand outside of science and are always purely subjective. One cannot, therefore, classify nations according to their worth and speak of them as worthy or less worthy. Consequently, the question whether or not the Russians are inferior lies completely outside the scope of our consideration. We do not at all contend that they are so. What we maintain is only that they do not *wish* to enter into the scheme of human social cooperation. In relation to human society and the community of nations their position is that of a people intent on nothing but the consumption of what others have accumulated. People among whom the ideas of Dostoyevsky, Tolstoy, and Lenin are a living force cannot produce a lasting social organization. They must revert to a condition of complete barbarism. Russia is endowed far more richly by nature with fertility of soil and mineral resources of all kinds than is the United States. If the Russians had pursued the same capitalistic policy as the Americans, they would today be the richest people in the world. Despotism, imperialism, and Bolshevism have made them the poorest. Now they are seeking capital and credits from all over the world.

Once this is recognized, it clearly follows what must be the guiding principle of the policy of the civilized nations toward Russia. Let the Russians be Russians. Let them do what they want in their own country. But do not let them pass beyond the boundaries of their own land to destroy European civilization. This is not to say, of course, that the importation and translation of Russian writings ought to be prohibited. Neurotics may enjoy them as much as they wish; the healthy will, in any case, eschew them. Nor does this mean that the Russians ought to be prohibited from spreading their propaganda and distributing bribes the way the Czars did throughout the world. If modern civilization were unable to defend itself against the attacks of hirelings, then it could not, in any case, remain in existence much longer. This is not to say, either, that Americans or Europeans ought to be prevented from visiting Russia if they are attracted to it. Let them view at first hand, at their own risk and on their own responsibility, the land of mass murder and mass misery. Nor does this mean that capitalists ought to be prevented from granting loans to the Soviets or otherwise to invest capital in Russia. If they are foolish enough to believe that they will ever see any part of it again, let them make the venture.

But the governments of Europe and America must stop promoting Soviet destructionism by paying premiums for exports to Soviet Russia and thereby furthering the Russian Soviet system by financial contributions. Let them stop propagandizing for emigration and the export of capital to Soviet Russia.

Whether or not the Russian people are to discard the Soviet system is for them to settle among themselves. The land of the knout and the prison-camp no longer poses a threat to the world today. With all their will to war and destruction, the Russians are no longer capable seriously of imperiling the peace of Europe. One may therefore safely let them alone. The only thing that needs to be resisted is any tendency on our part to support or promote the destructionist policy of the Soviets.

# 4

# Liberalism and
# the Political Parties

## 1. The "Doctrinairism" of the Liberals

Classical liberalism has been reproached with being too obstinate and not ready enough to compromise. It was because of its inflexibility that it was defeated in its struggle with the nascent anticapitalist parties of all kinds. If it had realized, as these other parties did, the importance of compromise and concession to popular slogans in winning the favor of the masses, it would have been able to preserve at least some of its influence. But it has never bothered to build for itself a party organization and a party machine as the anticapitalist parties have done. It has never attached any importance to political tactics in electoral campaigns and parliamentary proceedings. It has never gone in for scheming opportunism or political bargaining. This unyielding doctrinairism necessarily brought about the decline of liberalism.

The factual assertions contained in these statements are entirely in accordance with the truth, but to believe that they constitute a reproach against liberalism is to reveal a complete misunderstanding of its essential spirit. The ultimate and most profound of the fundamental insights of liberal thought is that it is ideas that constitute the foundation on which the whole edifice of human social cooperation is constructed and sustained and that a lasting social structure cannot be built on the basis of

155

false and mistaken ideas. Nothing can serve as a substitute for an ideology that enhances human life by fostering social cooperation—least of all lies, whether they be called "tactics," "diplomacy," or "compromise." If men will not, from a recognition of social necessity, voluntarily do what must be done if society is to be maintained and general well-being advanced, no one can lead them to the right path by any cunning stratagem or artifice. If they err and go astray, then one must endeavor to enlighten them by instruction. But if they cannot be enlightened, if they persist in error, then nothing can be done to prevent catastrophe. All the tricks and lies of demagogic politicians may well be suited to promote the cause of those who, whether in good faith or bad, work for the destruction of society. But the cause of social progress, the cause of the further development and intensification of social bonds, cannot be advanced by lies and demagogy. No power on earth, no crafty stratagem or clever deception could succeed in duping mankind into accepting a social doctrine that it not only does not acknowledge, but openly spurns.

The only way open to anyone who wishes to lead the world back to liberalism is to convince his fellow citizens of the necessity of adopting the liberal program. This work of enlightenment is the sole task that the liberal can and must perform in order to avert as much as lies within his power the destruction toward which society is rapidly heading today. There is no place here for concessions to any of the favorite or customary prejudices and errors. In regard to questions that will decide whether or not society is to continue to exist at all, whether millions of people are to prosper or perish, there is no room for compromise either from weakness or from misplaced deference for the sensibilities of others.

If liberal principles once again are allowed to guide the policies of great nations, if a revolution in public opinion could once more give capitalism free rein, the world will be able gradually to raise itself from the condition into which the policies of the combined anticapitalist factions have plunged it.

There is no other way out of the political and social chaos of the present age.

The most serious illusion under which classical liberalism labored was its optimism in regard to the direction that the evolution of society was bound to take. To the champions of liberalism—the sociologists and economists of the eighteenth and the first half of the nineteenth century and their supporters—it seemed certain that mankind would advance to ever higher stages of perfection and that nothing would be able to arrest this progress. They were firmly convinced that rational cognition of the fundamental laws of social cooperation and interdependence, which they had discovered, would soon become common and that thereafter the social bonds peacefully uniting mankind would become ever closer, there would be a progressive improvement in general well-being, and civilization would rise to ever higher levels of culture. Nothing could shake their optimism. As the attack on liberalism began to grow steadily fiercer, as the ascendancy of liberal ideas in politics was challenged from all sides, they thought that what they had to contend with was only the last volleys fired in retreat by a moribund system that did not require serious study and counterattack because it would in any case soon collapse of itself.

The liberals were of the opinion that all men have the intellectual capacity to reason correctly about the difficult problems of social cooperation and to act accordingly. They were so impressed with the clarity and self-evidence of the reasoning by which they had arrived at their political ideas that they were quite unable to understand how anyone could fail to comprehend it. They never grasped two facts: first, that the masses lack the capacity to think logically; and secondly, that in the eyes of most people, even when they are able to recognize the truth, a momentary, special advantage that may be enjoyed immediately appears more important than a lasting greater gain that must be deferred. Most people do not have even the intellectual endowments required to think through the—after all very complicated—problems of social cooperation, and they certainly do not have the will power necessary to make those provisional sacrifices that all social action demands. The slogans of interventionism and of socialism, especially proposals for the partial expropriation of private property, always find ready and enthusiastic approval with the masses, who expect to profit directly and immediately from them.

## 2. Political Parties

There can be no more grievous misunderstanding of the meaning and nature of liberalism than to think that it would be possible to secure the victory of liberal ideas by resorting to the methods employed today by the other political parties.

In a caste and status society, constituted not of citizens with equal rights, but divided into ranks vested with different duties and prerogatives, there are no political parties in the modern sense. As long as the special privileges and immunities of the different castes are not called into question, peace reigns among them. But once the privileges of caste and status are contested, the issue is joined, and civil war can be avoided only if one side or the other, recognizing its weakness, yields without an appeal to arms. In all such conflicts, the position of each individual is determined from the outset by his status as a member of one caste or another. To be sure, there can be renegades who, in the expectation of being better able to provide for their personal advantage on the side of the enemy, fight against the members of their own caste and are consequently viewed by them as traitors. But, apart from such exceptional cases, the individual is not confronted with the question of which of the opposing groups he ought to join. He stands by the members of his own caste and shares their fate. The caste or castes that are dissatisfied with their position rebel against the prevailing order and have to win their demands against the opposition of the others. The ultimate outcome of the conflict is—if everything does not, in fact, remain as it was because the rebels have been worsted— that the old order is replaced by a new one in which the rights of the various castes are different from what they were before.

With the advent of liberalism came the demand for the abolition of all special privileges. The society of caste and status had to make way for a new order in which there were to be only citizens with equal rights. What was under attack was no longer only the particular privileges of the different castes, but the very existence of all privileges. Liberalism tore down the barriers of rank and status and liberated man from the restrictions with which the old order had surrounded him. It was in capitalist society, under a system of government founded on liberal principles, that the individual was first granted the opportunity to participate directly in political life and was first called upon to make a personal decision in regard to political goals and ideals. In the caste and status society of earlier days, the only political conflicts had been those among the different castes, each of which had formed a solid front in opposition to the others; or, in the absence of such conflicts, there were, within those castes that were permitted a share in political life, factional conflicts among coteries and cliques for influence, power, and a place at the helm. Only under a polity in which all citizens enjoy equal rights—corresponding to the liberal ideal, which has nowhere ever been fully achieved—can there be political parties consisting of associations of persons who want to see their ideas on legislation and administration put into effect. For there can very well be differences of opinion concerning the best way to achieve the liberal aim of assuring peaceful social cooperation, and these differences of opinion must join issue as conflicts of ideas.

Thus, in a liberal society there could be socialist parties too. Even parties that seek to have a special legal position conceded to particular groups would not be impossible under a liberal system. But all these parties must acknowledge liberalism (at least temporarily, until they emerge victorious) so far as to make use in their political struggles solely of the weapons of the intellect, which liberalism views as the only ones permissible in such contests, even though, in the last analysis, as socialists or as champions of special privileges, the members of the antiliberal parties reject the liberal philosophy. Thus, some of the pre-Marxist "utopian" socialists fought for socialism within the framework of liberalism, and in the golden age of liberalism in western Europe, the clergy and the nobility tried to achieve their ends within the framework of a modern constitutional state.

The parties that we see at work today are of an entirely different kind. To be sure, some part of their program is concerned with the whole of society and purports to address itself to the problem of how social cooperation is to be achieved. But what this part of their program says is only a concession wrung from them by the liberal ideology. What they aim at in reality is set forth in another part of their program, which is the only part that they pay any attention to and which stands in irreconcilable contradiction to the part that is couched in terms of the general welfare. Present-day political parties are the champions not only of certain of the privileged orders of earlier days that desire to see preserved and extended traditional prerogatives that liberalism had to allow them to keep because its victory was not complete, but also of certain groups that strive for special privileges, that is to say, that desire to attain the status of a caste. Liberalism addresses itself to all and proposes a program acceptable to all alike. It promises no one privileges. By calling for the renunciation of the pursuit of special interests, it even demands sacrifices, though, of course, only provisional ones, involving the giving up of a relatively small advantage in order to attain a greater one. But the parties of special interests address themselves only to a part of society. To this part, for which alone they intend to work, they promise special advantages at the expense of the rest of society.

All modern political parties and all modern party ideologies originated as a reaction on the part of special group interests fighting for a privileged status against liberalism. Before the rise of liberalism, there were, of course, privileged orders with their special interests and prerogatives and their mutual conflicts, but at that time the ideology of the status society could still express itself in a completely naive and unembarrassed way. In the conflicts that occurred in those days between the champions and the opponents of special privilege, there was never any question of the antisocial character of the whole system nor any need of maintaining the pretense of justifying it on social grounds. One cannot, therefore, draw any direct comparison between the old system of privileged orders and the activities and propaganda of the present-day parties of special interests.

To understand the true character of all these parties, one must keep in mind the fact that they were originally formed solely as a defense of special privileges against the teachings of liberalism. Their party doctrines are not, like those of liberalism, the political application of a comprehensive, carefully thought-out theory of society. The political ideology of liberalism was derived from a fundamental system of ideas that had first been developed as a scientific theory without any thought of its political significance. In contradistinction to this, the special rights and privileges sought by the antiliberal parties were, from the very outset, already realized in existing social institutions, and it was in justification of the latter that one undertook subsequently to elaborate an ideology, a task that was generally treated as a matter of little moment that could easily be disposed of with a few brief words. Farm groups think it sufficient to point out the indispensability of agriculture. The trade unions appeal to the indispensability of labor. The parties of the middle class cite the importance of the existence of a social stratum that represents the golden mean. It seems to trouble them little that such appeals contribute nothing to proving the necessity or even the advantageousness to the general public of the special privileges they are striving for. The groups that they desire to win over will follow them in any case, and as for the others, every attempt at recruiting supporters from their ranks would be futile.

Thus, all these modern parties of special interests, no matter how far apart their goals may diverge or how violently they may contend against one another, form a united front in the battle against liberalism. In the eyes of all of them, the principle of liberalism that the rightly understood interests of all men are, in the long run, compatible is like a red cloth waved in front of a bull. As they see it, there are irreconcilable conflicts of interests that can be settled only by the victory of one faction over the others, to the advantage of the former and the disadvantage of the latter. Liberalism, these parties assert, is not what it pretends to be. It too is nothing but a party program seeking to champion the special interests of a particular group, the bourgeoisie, i.e., the capitalists and entrepreneurs, against the interests of all other groups.

The fact that this allegation forms part of the propaganda of Marxism accounts for much of the latter's success. If the doctrine of the irreconcilable conflict between the interests of different classes within a society based on private ownership of the means of production is taken as the essential dogma of Marxism, then all the parties active today on the European continent would have to be considered as Marxist. The doctrine of class antagonisms and of class conflict is also accepted by the nationalist parties in so far as they share the opinion that these antagonisms do exist in capitalist society and that the conflicts to which they give rise must run their course. What distinguishes them from the Marxist parties is only that they wish to overcome class conflict by reverting to a status society constituted along the lines that they recommend and by shifting the battlefront to the international arena, where they believe it should be. They do not dispute the statement that conflicts of this kind occur in a society based on private ownership of the means of production. They merely contend that such antagonisms ought not to arise, and in order to eliminate them, they want to guide and regulate private property by acts of government interference; they want interventionism in place of capitalism. But, in the last analysis, this is in no way different from what the Marxists say. They too promise to lead the world to a new social order in which there will be no more classes, class antagonisms, or class conflicts.

In order to grasp the meaning of the doctrine of the class war, one must bear in mind that it is directed against the liberal doctrine of the harmony of the rightly understood interests of all members of a free society founded on the principle of private ownership of the means of production. The liberals maintained that with the elimination of all the artificial distinctions of caste and status, the abolition of all privileges, and the establishment of equality before the law, nothing else stands in the way of the peaceful cooperation of all members of society, because then their rightly understood, long-run interests coincide. All the objections that the champions of feudalism, of special privileges, and of distinctions of caste and status sought to advance against this doctrine soon proved quite unjustified and were unable to gain any notable support. But in Ricardo's system of catallactics one may find the point of departure for a new theory of the conflict of interests within the capitalist system. Ricardo believed that he could show how, in the course of progressive economic development, a shift takes place in the relations among the three forms of income in his system, viz., profit, rent, and wages. It was this that impelled a few English writers in the third and fourth decades of the nineteenth century to speak of the three classes of capitalists, landowners, and wage-laborers and to maintain that an irreconcilable antagonism exists among these groups. This line of thought was later taken up by Marx.

In the *Communist Manifesto,* Marx still did not distinguish between caste and class. Only later, when he became acquainted in London with the writings of the forgotten pamphleteers of the twenties and thirties and, under their influence, began the study of Ricardo's system, did he realize that the problem in this case was to show that even in a society without caste distinctions and privileges irreconcilable conflicts still exist. This antagonism of interests he deduced from Ricardo's system by distinguishing among the three classes of capitalists, landowners, and workers. But he by no means adhered firmly to this distinction. Sometimes he asserts that there are only two classes, the propertied and the propertyless; at other times he distinguishes among more classes than just the two or three great ones. At no time, however, did Marx or any one of his many followers attempt in any way to define the concept and nature of the classes. It is significant that the chapter entitled "The Classes" in the third volume of *Capital* breaks off after a few sentences. More than a generation elapsed from the appearance of the *Communist Manifesto,* in which Marx first makes class antagonism and class war the keystone of his entire doctrine, to the time of his death. During this entire period Marx wrote volume after volume, but he never came to the point of explaining what is to be understood by a "class." In his treatment of the problem of classes Marx never went beyond the mere statement, without any proof, of a dogma or, let us rather say, of a slogan.

In order to prove that the doctrine of class warfare is true, one would have to be able to establish two facts: on the one hand, that there is an identity of interests among the members of each class; and, on the other hand, that what benefits one class injures the other. This, however, has never been accomplished. Indeed, it has never even been attempted. Precisely because "class comrades" are all in the same "social situation," there is no identity of interests among them, but rather competition. The worker, for example, who is employed under better-than-average conditions has an interest in excluding competitors who could reduce his income to the average level. In the decades when the doctrine of the international solidarity of the proletariat was proclaimed time and time again in verbose resolutions adopted at the international Marxist congresses, the workers of the United States and Australia set up the greatest obstacles to immigration. By means of a complex network of petty regulations, the English trade unions made impossible the entrance of outsiders into their branches of labor. What has been done by the labor parties in this regard in every country during the last few years is well known. Of course, one can say that this ought not to have happened; the workers ought to have acted differently; what they did was wrong. But one cannot deny that it directly served their interests—at least for the moment.

Liberalism has demonstrated that the antagonism of interests, which, according to a widely prevalent opinion, is supposed to exist among different persons, groups, and strata within a society based on private ownership of the means of production, does not, in fact, occur. Any increase in total capital raises the income of capitalists and landowners absolutely and that of workers both absolutely and relatively. As regards their income, any shifts in the various interests of the different groups and strata of society— the entrepreneurs, capitalists, landowners, and workers—occur together and move in the same direction as they pass through different phases in their fluctuations; what varies is only the ratio of their shares of the social product. The interests of the landowners oppose those of the members of the other groups only in the one case of a genuine monopoly of a certain mineral. The interests of the entrepreneurs can never diverge from those of the consumers. The entrepreneur prospers the better, the better he is able to anticipate the desires of the consumers.

Conflicts of interests can occur only in so far as restrictions on the owners' free disposal of the means of production are imposed by the interventionist policy of the government or by interference on the part of other social forces armed with coercive power. For example, the price of a certain article can be artificially raised by a protective tariff, or the wages of a certain group of workers can be increased by excluding all competitors for their jobs. The famous line of reasoning of the free-trade school, never refuted and forever irrefutable, applies to cases of this kind. Such special privileges can, of course, benefit the particular group on whose behalf they were instituted only if other groups have been unable to win similar privileges for themselves. But it cannot be assumed that it would be possible, in the long run, to deceive the majority of the people about the real significance of such special privileges so that they will tolerate them willingly. Yet if one undertakes to use force to compel their acceptance, one will provoke violent rebellion—in short, a disturbance of the peaceful course of social cooperation, the preservation of which is in the interest of everyone. If one seeks to solve the problem by making these special privileges, not exceptions on behalf of just one or a few persons, groups, or strata of society, but the general rule, as, for example, by resorting to import duties to protect most of the articles sold on the home market, or by using similar measures to bar access to the majority of occupations, the advantages gained by each particular group are counterbalanced by the disadvantages that they must suffer, and the end result is only that all are injured by the consequent lowering of the productivity of labor.

If one rejects this doctrine of liberalism, if one heaps ridicule on the controversial theory of the "harmony of interests of all men," then it is not true, either, as is wrongly assumed by all schools of antiliberal thought, that there could still be a solidarity of interests within narrower circles, as, for instance, among members of the same nation (as against other nations) or among members of the same "class" (as against other classes). In order to demonstrate the existence of such an alleged solidarity, a special line of reasoning would be necessary that no one has followed or has even attempted to follow. For all the arguments that could be employed to prove the existence of a solidarity of interests among the members of any of these groups prove much more besides, viz., the universal solidarity of interests within ecumenical society. How those apparent conflicts of interest that seem at first sight to be irreconcilable are in fact resolved can be shown only by means of a line of reasoning that treats all mankind as an essentially harmonious community and allows no room for the demonstration of any irreconcilable antagonisms among nations, classes, races, and the like.

The antiliberal parties do not, as they believe, prove that there is any solidarity of interests within nations, classes, races, etc. All that they actually do is to recommend to the members of these particular groups alliances for a common struggle against all other groups. When they speak of a solidarity of interests within these groups, they are not so much affirming a fact as stating a postulate. In reality, they are not saying, "The interests are identical," but rather, "The interests ought to be made identical by an alliance for united action."

The modern parties of special interests declare quite frankly and unequivocally, from the very outset, that the aim of their policy is the creation of special privileges for a particular group. Agrarian parties strive for protective tariffs and other advantages (e.g., subsidies) for farmers; civil service parties aim at securing privileges for bureaucrats; regional parties are dedicated to gaining special advantages for the inhabitants of a certain region. All these parties evidently seek nothing but the advantage of a single group in society, without consideration of the whole of society or of all other groups, however much they may seek to palliate their procedure by declaring that the welfare of the whole of society can be achieved only by furthering the interests of agriculture, the civil service, etc. Indeed, their exclusive concern with but a single segment of society and their labors and endeavors on its behalf alone have become increasingly obvious and more cynical with the passage of the years. When the modern antiliberal movements were still in their infancy, they had to be more circumspect in regard to such matters, because the generation that had been reared on the liberal philosophy had learned to look upon the undisguised advocacy of the special interests of various groups as antisocial.

The champions of special interests can form great parties only by composing a single combat unit out of the combined forces of various groups whose special interests are in conflict. Privileges granted to a particular group, however, have practical value only when they accrue to a minority and are not outweighed by the privileges granted to another group. But unless circumstances are exceptionally favorable, a small group cannot hope at present, while the liberal condemnation of the privileges of the nobility still retains some traces of its earlier influence, to be able to have their claim to be treated as a privileged class prevail against all other groups. The problem of all the parties of special interests, therefore, is to form great parties out of relatively small groups with differing and, indeed, directly conflicting interests. But in view of the mentality that leads these smaller parties to put forth and defend their demands for special privileges, it is quite impracticable to achieve this end by way of an open alliance among the various groups. No provisional sacrifice can be asked of the man who strives for the acquisition of a privileged position for his own group or even for himself alone; if he were capable of understanding the reason for making the provisional sacrifice, then he would certainly think along liberal lines and not in terms of the demands of those engaged in the scramble for special privileges. Nor can one openly tell him that he will gain more from the privilege intended for him than he will lose from the privileges that he will have to concede to others, for any speeches and writings to this effect could not, in the long run, remain hidden from the others and would impel them to raise their demands even higher.

Thus, the parties of special interests are obliged to be cautious. In speaking of this most important point in their endeavors, they must resort to ambiguous expressions intended to obscure the true state of affairs. Protectionist parties are the best example of this kind of equivocation. They must always be careful to represent the interest in the protective tariffs they recommend as that of a wider group. When associations of manufacturers advocate protective tariffs, the party leaders generally take care not to mention that the interests of individual groups and often even of individual concerns are by no means identical and harmonious. The weaver is injured by tariffs on machines and yarn and will promote the protectionist movement only in the expectation that textile tariffs will be high enough to compensate him for the loss that he suffers from the other tariffs. The farmer who grows fodder demands tariffs on fodder, which the cattle raisers oppose; the winegrower demands a tariff on wine, which is just as disadvantageous to the farmer who does not happen to cultivate a vineyard as it is to the urban consumer. Nevertheless, the protectionists appear as a single party united behind a common program. This is made possible only by throwing a veil of obscurity over the truth of the matter.

Any attempt to found a party of special interests on the basis of an equal apportionment of privileges among the majority of the population would be utterly senseless. A privilege accruing to the majority ceases to be such. In a predominantly agricultural country, which exports farm products, an agrarian party working for special favors for farmers would be, in the long run, impossible. What should it demand? Protective tariffs could not benefit these farmers, who must export; and subsidies could not be paid to the majority of producers, because the minority could not provide them. The minority, on the other hand, which demands privileges for itself must induce the illusion that great masses stand behind it. When the agrarian parties in the industrial countries present their demands, they include in what they call the "farm population" landless workers, cottagers, and owners of small plots of land, who have no interest in a protective tariff on agricultural products. When the labor parties make some demand on behalf of a group of workers, they always talk of the great mass of the working people and gloss over the fact that the interests of trade-unionists employed in different branches of production are not identical, but, on the contrary, actually antagonistic, and that even within individual industries and concerns there are sharp conflicts of interest.

This is one of the two fundamental weaknesses of all parties aiming at privileges on behalf of special interests. On the one hand, they are obliged to rely on only a small group, because privileges cease to be privileges when they are granted to the majority; but, on the other hand, it is only in their guise as the champions and representatives of the majority that they have any prospect of realizing their demands. The fact that many parties in different countries have sometimes succeeded in overcoming this difficulty in carrying on their propaganda and have managed to imbue each social stratum or group with the conviction that its members may expect special advantages from the triumph of the party speaks only for the diplomatic and tactical skill of the leadership and for the want of judgment and the political immaturity of the voting masses. It by no means proves that a real solution of the problem is, in fact, possible. Of course, one can simultaneously promise city-dwellers cheaper bread and farmers higher prices for grain, but one cannot keep both promises at the same time. It is easy enough to promise one group that one will support an increase in certain government expenditures without a corresponding reduction in other government expenditures, and at the same time hold out to another group the prospect of lower taxes; but one cannot keep both these promises at the same time either. The technique of these parties is based on the division of society into producers and consumers. They are also wont to make use of the usual hypostasis of the state in questions of fiscal policy that enables them to advocate new expenditures to be paid out of the public treasury without any particular concern on their part over how such expenses are to be defrayed, and at the same time to complain about the heavy burden of taxes.

The other basic defect of these parties is that the demands they raise for each particular group are limitless. There is, in their eyes, only *one* limit to the quantity to be demanded: the resistance put up by the other side. This is entirely in keeping with their character as parties striving for privileges on behalf of special interests. Yet parties that follow no definite program, but come into conflict in the pursuit of unlimited desires for privileges on behalf of some and for legal disabilities for others, must bring about the destruction of every political system. People have been coming to recognize this ever more clearly and have begun to speak of a crisis of the modern state and of a crisis of the parliamentary system. In reality, what is involved is a crisis of the ideologies of the modern parties of special interests.

### 3. *The Crisis of Parliamentarism and the Idea of a Diet Representing Special Groups*

Parliamentarism, as it has slowly developed in England and in some of her colonies since the seventeenth century, and on the European continent since the overthrow of Napoleon and the July and February Revolutions, presupposes the general acceptance of the ideology of liberalism. All who enter a parliament charged with the responsibility of there deciding how the country shall be governed must be imbued with the conviction that the rightly understood interests of all parts and members of society coincide and that every kind of special privilege for particular groups and classes of the population is detrimental to the common good and must be eliminated. The different parties in a parliament empowered to perform the functions assigned to it by all the constitutions of recent times may, of course, take different sides in regard to particular political questions, but they must consider themselves as the representatives of the whole nation, not as representatives of particular districts or social strata. Above all their differences of opinion there must prevail the conviction that, in the last analysis, they are united by a common purpose and an identical aim and that only the means to the attainment of the goal toward which they all aspire are in dispute. The parties are not separated by an unbridgeable gulf nor by conflicts of interests that they are prepared to carry on to the bitter end even if this means that the whole nation must suffer and the country be brought to ruin. What divides the parties is the position they take in regard to concrete problems of policy. There are, therefore, only two parties: the party in power and the one that wants to be in power. Even the opposition does not seek to obtain power in order to promote certain interests or to fill official posts with its party members, but in order to translate its ideas into legislation and to put them into effect in the administration of the country.

Only under these conditions are parliaments or parliamentary governments practicable. For a time they were realized in the Anglo-Saxon countries, and some traces of them can still be found there today. On the European continent, even during the period usually characterized as the golden age of liberalism, one could really speak only of a certain approximation to these conditions. For decades now, conditions in the popular assemblies of Europe have been something like their direct opposite. There are a great number of parties, and each particular party is itself divided into various subgroups, which generally present a united front to the outside world, but usually oppose one another within the party councils as vehemently as they oppose the other parties publicly. Each particular party and faction feels itself appointed to be the sole champion of certain special interests, which it undertakes to lead to victory at any cost. To allot as much as possible from the public coffers to "our own," to favor them by protective tariffs, immigration barriers, "social legislation," and privileges of all kinds, at the expense of the rest of society, is the whole sum and substance of their policy.

As their demands are, in principle, limitless, it is impossible for any one of these parties ever to achieve all the ends it envisages. It is unthinkable that what the agrarian or labor parties strive for could ever be entirely realized. Every party seeks, nevertheless, to attain to such influence as will permit it to satisfy its desires as far as possible, while also taking care always to be able to justify to its electors why all their wishes could not be fulfilled. This can be done either by seeking to give in public the appearance of being in the opposition, although the party is actually in power, or by striving to shift the blame to some force not answerable to its influence: the sovereign, in the monarchical state; or, under certain circumstances, foreign powers or the like. The Bolsheviks cannot make Russia happy nor the socialists Austria because "western capitalism" prevents it. For at least fifty years antiliberal parties have ruled in Germany and Austria, yet we still read in their manifestoes and public statements, even in those of their "scientific" champions, that all existing evils are to be blamed on the dominance of "liberal" principles.

A parliament composed of the supporters of the antiliberal parties of special interests is not capable of carrying on its business and must, in the long run, disappoint everyone. This is what people mean today and have meant for many years now when they speak of the crisis of parliamentarism.

As the solution for this crisis, some demand the abolition of democracy and the parliamentary system and the institution of a dictatorship. We do not propose to discuss once again the objections to dictatorship. This we have already done in sufficient detail.

A second suggestion is directed toward remedying the alleged deficiencies of a general assembly composed of members elected directly by all the citizens, by either supplementing or replacing it altogether with a diet composed of delegates chosen by autonomous corporative bodies or guilds formed by the different branches of trade, industry, and the professions. The members of a general popular assembly, it is said, lack the requisite objectivity and the knowledge of economic affairs. What is needed is not so much a general policy as an economic policy. The representatives of industrial and professional guilds would be able to come to an agreement on questions whose solution either eludes entirely the delegates of constituencies formed on a merely geographical basis or becomes apparent to them only after long delay.

In regard to an assembly composed of delegates representing different occupational associations, the crucial question about which one must be clear is how a vote is to be taken, or, if each member is to have one vote, how many representatives are to be granted to each guild. This is a problem that must be resolved before the diet convenes; but once this question is settled, one can spare oneself the trouble of calling the assembly into session, for the outcome of the voting is thereby already determined. To be sure, it is quite another question whether the distribution of power among the guilds, once established, can be maintained. It will always be—let us not cherish any delusions on this score— unacceptable to the majority of the people. In order to create a parliament acceptable to the majority, there is no need of an assembly divided along occupational lines. Everything will depend on whether the discontent aroused by the policies adopted by the deputies of the guilds is great enough to lead to the violent over-throw of the whole system. In contrast to the democratic system, this one offers no guarantee that a change in policy desired by the overwhelming majority of the population will take place. In saying this, we have said everything that needs to be said against the idea of an assembly constituted on the basis of occupational divisions. For the liberal, any system which does not exclude every violent interruption of peaceful development is, from the very outset, out of the question.

Many supporters of the idea of a diet composed of guild representatives think that conflicts should be settled, not by the submission of one faction to another, but by the mutual adjust-ment of differences. But what is supposed to happen if the parties cannot succeed in reaching agreement? Compromises come about only when the threatening spectre of an unfavorable issue induces each party to the dispute to make some concession. No one prevents the different parties from coming to an agreement even in a parliament composed of delegates elected directly by the whole nation. No one will be able to compel agreement in a diet consisting of deputies chosen by the members of occupational associations.

Thus, an assembly so constituted cannot function like a parliament that serves as the organ of a democratic system. It cannot be the place where differences of political opinion are peacefully adjusted. It is not in a position to prevent the violent interruption of the peaceful progress of society by insurrection, revolution, and civil war. For the crucial decisions that determine the distribution of political power in the state are not made within its chambers or during the elections that decide its composition. The decisive factor in determining the distribution of power is the relative weight assigned by the constitution to the different corporate associations in the shaping of public policy. But this is a matter that is decided outside the chambers of the diet and without any organic relationship to the elections by which its members are chosen.

It is therefore quite correct to withhold the name "parliament" from an assembly consisting of representatives of corporate associations organized along occupational lines. Political terminology has been accustomed, in the last two centuries, to make a sharp distinction between a parliament and such an assembly. If one does not wish to confound all the concepts of political science, one does well to adhere to this distinction.

Sidney and Beatrice Webb, as well as a number of syndicalists and guild socialists, following in this respect recommendations already made in earlier days by many continental advocates of a reform in the upper chamber, have proposed letting two chambers exist side by side, one elected directly by the whole nation, and the other composed of deputies elected from constituencies divided along occupational lines. However, it is obvious that this suggestion in no way remedies the defects of the system of guild representation. In practice, the bicameral system can function only if one house has the upper hand and has the unconditional power to impose its will on the other, or if, when the two chambers take different positions on an issue, an attempt at a compromise solution must be made. In the absence of such an attempt, however, the conflict remains to be settled outside the chambers of parliament, in the last resort by force alone. Twist and turn the problem as one will, one always returns in the end to the same insurmountable difficulties. Such are the stumbling blocks on which all proposals of this and a similar kind must come to grief, whether they are called corporativism, guild socialism, or anything else. The impracticability of these schemes is admitted when people finally content themselves by recommending a completely inconsequential innovation: the establishment of an economic council empowered to serve solely in an advisory capacity.

The champions of the idea of an assembly composed of guild deputies labor under a serious delusion if they think that the antagonisms that today rend the fabric of national unity can be overcome by dividing the population and the popular assembly along occupational lines. One cannot get rid of these antagonisms by tinkering with technicalities in the constitution. They can be overcome only by the liberal ideology.

## 4. *Liberalism and the Parties of Special Interests*

The parties of special interests, which see nothing more in politics than the securing of privileges and prerogatives for their own groups, not only make the parliamentary system impossible; they rupture the unity of the state and of society. They lead not merely to the crisis of parliamentarism, but to a general political and social crisis. Society cannot, in the long run, exist if it is divided into sharply defined groups, each intent on wresting special privileges for its own members, continually on the alert to see that it does not suffer any setback, and prepared, at any moment, to sacrifice the most important political institutions for the sake of winning some petty advantage.

To the parties of special interests, all political questions appear exclusively as problems of political tactics. Their ultimate goal is fixed for them from the start. Their aim is to obtain, at the cost of the rest of the population, the greatest possible advantages and privileges for the groups they represent. The party platform is intended to disguise this objective and give it a certain appearance of justification, but under no circumstances to announce it publicly as the goal of party policy. The members of the party, in any case, know what their goal is; they do not need to have it explained to them. How much of it ought to be imparted to the world is, however, a purely tactical question.

All antiliberal parties want nothing but to secure special favors for their own members, in complete disregard of the resulting disintegration of the whole structure of society. They cannot withstand for a moment the criticism that liberalism makes of their aims. They cannot deny, when their demands are subjected to the test of logical scrutiny, that their activity, in the last analysis, has antisocial and destructive effects and that even on the most cursory examination it must prove impossible for any social order to arise from the operations of parties of special interests continually working against one another. To be sure, the obviousness of these facts has not been able to damage the parties of special interests in the eyes of those who lack the capacity to look beyond the immediate present. The great mass of people do not inquire what will happen the day after tomorrow or later on. They think of today and, at most, of the next day. They do not ask what must follow if all other groups too, in the pursuit of their special interests, were to display the same unconcern for the general welfare. They hope to succeed not only in realizing their own demands, but also in beating down those of others. For the few who apply higher standards to the activities of political parties, who demand that even in political action the categorical imperative be followed ("Act only on that principle which you can will at the same time to be a universal law, i.e., so that no contradiction results from the attempt to conceive of your action as a law to be universally complied with"), the ideology of the parties of special interests certainly has nothing to offer.

Socialism has gained a considerable advantage from this logical deficiency in the position adopted by the parties of special interests. For many who are unable to grasp the great ideal of liberalism, but who think too clearly to be content with demands for privileged treatment on behalf of particular groups, the principle of socialism took on a special significance. The idea of a socialist society—to which one cannot, in spite of its necessarily inherent defects, which we have already discussed in detail, deny a certain grandeur of conception—served to conceal and, at the same time, to vindicate the weakness of the position taken by the parties of special interests. It had the effect of diverting the attention of the critic from the activities of the party to a great problem, which, whatever one may think of it, was at all events deserving of serious and exhaustive consideration.

In the last hundred years, the socialist ideal, in one form or another, has found adherents among many sincere and honest people. A number of the best and noblest men and women have accepted it with enthusiasm. It has been the guiding star of distinguished statesmen. It has achieved a dominant position at the universities and has served as a source of inspiration to youth. It has so filled the thoughts and fed the emotions of both the past and the present generation that history will some day quite justly characterize our era as the age of socialism. In the last decades, in all countries people have done as much as they could to make the socialist ideal a reality by nationalizing and municipalizing enterprises and by adopting measures designed to lead to a planned economy. The defects necessarily involved in socialist management—its unfavorable effects on the productivity of human labor and the impossibility of economic calculation under socialism—everywhere brought these endeavors to the point where virtually every step further in the direction of socialism threatened too flagrant an impairment of the supply of goods available to the public. From sheer necessity one had to pause on the road to socialism; and the socialist ideal—even while preserving its ideological ascendancy—became, in practical politics, merely a cloak for the labor parties in their scramble for privileges.

This could be shown to be true of each of the many socialist parties, such as, for instance, the various factions among the Christian socialists. We propose, however, to confine our discussion to the case of the Marxian socialists, who undoubtedly were and are the most important socialist party.

Marx and his followers were really serious about socialism. Marx rejected all those measures on behalf of particular groups and strata of society that are demanded by the parties of special interests. He did not dispute the validity of the liberal argument that the outcome of such acts of interference can only be a general reduction in the productivity of labor. When he thought, wrote, and spoke consistently, he always took the position that every attempt to tamper with the mechanism of the capitalist system by acts of intervention on the part of the government or of other social organs armed with the same coercive power is pointless because it does not bring about the result intended by its advocates, but instead reduces the productivity of the economy. Marx wanted to organize the workers for the conflict that would lead to the establishment of socialism, but not for the achievement of certain special privileges within a society still based on private ownership of the means of production. He wanted a socialist labor party, but not, as he put it, a "petty-bourgeois" party aiming at individual, piecemeal reforms.

Prevented by blind adherence to the preconceptions of his scholastic system from taking an unbiased view of things as they are, he thought that the workers, whom the writers under his intellectual influence had organized into "socialist" parties, would be content to stand by quietly watching the evolution of the capitalist system according to doctrine, so as not to postpone the day when it would be fully ripe for the expropriation of the expropriators and would "turn into" socialism. He did not see that the labor parties, just like the other parties of special interests that were simultaneously springing up everywhere, while acknowledging the socialist program as correct in principle, in practical politics were concerned only with the immediate goal of winning special privileges for the workers. The Marxist theory of the solidarity of the interests of all workers, which Marx had developed with quite other political ends in view, rendered excellent service in skillfully concealing the fact that the costs of the victories won by some groups of workers had to be borne by other groups of workers; that is to say, that in the field of allegedly "prolabor" legislation, as well as in trade-union struggles, the interests of the proletarians by no means coincide. In this respect, the Marxist doctrine performed the same service for the party championing the special interests of the workers as was accomplished for the German Centrist and other clerical parties by the appeal to religion; for the nationalist parties, by the appeal to national solidarity; for the agrarian parties, by the contention that the interests of the various groups of agricultural producers are identical; and for the protectionist parties, by the doctrine of the necessity of a comprehensive tariff for the protection of national labor. The more the social-democratic parties grew, the stronger became the influence of the trade unions within them and the more they became an association of trade unions that saw everything from the point of view of the closed shop and the increase of wages.

Liberalism does not have the least thing in common with any of these parties. It stands at the very opposite pole from all of them. It promises special favors to no one. It demands from everyone sacrifices on behalf of the preservation of society. These sacrifices—or, more accurately, the renunciation of immediately attainable advantages—are, to be sure, merely provisional; they quickly pay for themselves in greater and more lasting gains. Nevertheless, for the time being, they are sacrifices. Because of this, liberalism finds itself, from the very outset, in a peculiar position in the competition among parties. The antiliberal candidate promises special privileges to every particular group of voters: higher prices to the producers and lower prices to the consumers; higher salaries to public officeholders and lower taxes to taxpayers. He is prepared to agree to any desired expenditure at the cost of the public treasury or of the rich. No group is too small for him to disdain to seek its favor by a gift from the pocket of the "general public." The liberal candidate can only say to all voters that the pursuit of such special favors is antisocial.

## 5. Party Propaganda and Party Organization

When liberal ideas began to spread to central and eastern Europe from their homeland in western Europe, the traditional powers—the monarchy, the nobility, and the clergy—trusting in the instruments of repression that were at their disposal, felt completely safe. They did not consider it necessary to combat liberalism and the mentality of the Enlightenment with intellectual weapons. Suppression, persecution, and imprisonment of the malcontents seemed to them to be more serviceable. They boasted of the violent and coercive machinery of the army and the police. Too late they realized with horror that the new ideology snatched these weapons from their hands by conquering the minds of officials and soldiers. It took the defeat suffered by the old regime in the battle against liberalism to teach its adherents the truth that there is nothing in the world more powerful than ideologies and ideologists and that only with ideas can one fight against ideas. They realized that it is foolish to rely on arms, since one can deploy armed men only if they are prepared to obey, and that the basis of all power and dominion is, in the last analysis, ideological.

The acknowledgment of this sociological truth was one of the fundamental convictions on which the political theory of liberalism was based. From it liberalism had drawn no other conclusion than that, in the long run, truth and righteousness must triumph because their victory in the realm of ideas cannot be doubted. And whatever is victorious in this realm must ultimately succeed in the world of affairs as well, since no persecution is capable of suppressing it. It is therefore superfluous to trouble oneself especially about the spread of liberalism. Its victory is, in any case, certain.

The opponents of liberalism can be understood even in this respect only if one keeps in mind that their actions are nothing but the reverse of what liberalism teaches; that is, they are based on the rejection of and reaction against liberal ideas. They were not in a position to offer a comprehensive and consistent body of social and economic doctrine in opposition to the liberal ideology, for liberalism is the only possible conclusion that can be validly drawn from such a doctrine. Yet a program that promised something to only one group or a few groups had no chance of winning general support and was doomed from the outset to political failure. Thus, these parties had no other recourse than to hit upon some arrangement that would bring the groups to whom they addressed themselves completely under their sway and to keep them that way. They had to take care that liberal ideas found no adherents among the classes on which they depended.

To this end, they created party organizations that hold the individual so tightly in their grip that he dare not even think of resigning. In Germany and Austria, where this system was developed with pedantic thoroughness, and in the countries of eastern Europe, where it was copied, the individual is today no longer primarily a citizen, but a party member. Already as a child he is taken care of by the party. Sports and social activities are organized on partisan lines. The farmers' cooperative system, through whose intervention alone the farmer can lay claim to his share of the subsidies and grants accruing to agricultural producers; the institutions for the advancement of the professional classes; and the workingmen's labor exchange and savings bank system are all managed along party lines. In all matters on which the authorities are free to use their discretion, the individual, in order to be respected, requires the support of his party. Under such circumstances, laxity in party affairs leads to suspicion, but resignation means serious economic detriment, if not ruination and social ostracism.

The parties of special interests reserve for the problem of the professional classes a treatment peculiar to it alone. The independent professions of the lawyer, the doctor, the writer, and the artist are not represented in sufficiently great number to permit them to figure as parties of special interests in their own right. They are therefore the least open to the influence of the ideology of special class privileges. Their members clung longest and most stubbornly to liberalism. They had nothing to gain from adopting a policy of ruthless and unyielding struggle for the promotion of their particular interests. This was a situation that the parties working on behalf of organized pressure groups viewed with the utmost misgiving. They could not tolerate the intelligentsia's continued adherence to liberalism. For they feared that their own ranks might be thinned if liberal ideas, once again developed and expounded by a few individuals in these groups, were to gain enough strength to find acceptance and approval among the mass of their members. They had just learned how dangerous such ideologies could be to the prerogatives of the privileged orders of the caste and status society. The parties of special interests therefore proceeded systematically to organize themselves in such a way as to make the members of the "liberal" professions dependent on them. This was soon achieved by incorporating them into the mechanism of the party machinery. The doctor, the lawyer, the writer, the artist must enroll themselves in and subordinate themselves to the organization of their patients, clients, readers, and patrons. Whoever holds back or openly rebels is boycotted into compliance.

The subjugation of the independent professional classes finds its complement in the procedure followed in making appointments to teaching positions and to posts in the civil service. Where the party system is fully developed, only party members are appointed, whether of the one currently in power or of all the parties of special interests in accordance with an arrangement, tacit though it may be, arrived at among themselves. And ultimately even the independent press is brought under control by the threat of a boycott.

A crowning stroke in the organization of these parties was the establishment of their own bands of armed men. Organized in military fashion, after the pattern of the national army, they have drawn up their mobilization and operational plans, have weapons at their disposal, and are ready to strike. With their banners and brass bands they march through the streets heralding to the world the dawn of an era of endless agitation and warfare.

Two circumstances have so far served to mitigate the dangers of this situation. In the first place, a certain balance of power among the party forces has been reached in some of the more important countries. Where this is lacking, as in Russia and Italy, the power of the state, in disregard of the few remaining liberal principles that the rest of the world still acknowledges, is used to suppress and persecute the adherents of the opposition parties.

The second circumstance that, for the moment, still prevents the worst from happening is that even nations imbued with hostility toward liberalism and capitalism count on capital investment from the lands that have been the classical exemplars of the liberal and capitalist mentality—above all, the United States. Without these credits, the consequences of the policy of capital consumption that they have been pursuing would have already become much more obvious. Anticapitalism can maintain itself in existence only by sponging on capitalism. It must therefore take into consideration to a certain extent the public opinion of the West, where liberalism is still acknowledged today, even though in a much diluted form. In the fact that capitalists generally desire to lend only to such borrowers as hold out some prospect of repaying the loan, the destructionist parties profess to see that "world ascendancy of capital" about which they raise such a hue and cry.

### 6. *Liberalism as the "Party of Capital"*

Thus, it is easily seen that liberalism cannot be put into the same class with the parties of special interests without denying its very nature. It is something radically different from them all. They are out for battle and extol violence; liberalism, on the contrary, desires peace and the ascendancy of ideas. It is for this reason that all parties, however badly disunited they may otherwise be, form a united front against liberalism.

The enemies of liberalism have branded it as the party of the special interests of the capitalists. This is characteristic of their mentality. They simply cannot understand a political ideology as anything but the advocacy of certain special privileges opposed to the general welfare.

One cannot look on liberalism as a party of special interests, privileges, and prerogatives, because private ownership of the means of production is not a privilege redounding to the exclusive advantage of the capitalists, but an institution in the interest of the whole of society and consequently an institution that benefits everyone. This is the opinion not only of the liberals, but even, up to a certain point, of their opponents. When the Marxists champion the view that socialism cannot be made a reality until the world is "ripe" for it, because a social system never becomes extinct before "all the productive forces have developed for which it is broad enough," they concede, at least for the present, the social indispensability of the institution of private property. Even the Bolsheviks, who only a little while ago propagated with fire, sword, and the gallows their interpretation of Marxism—that is, that "ripeness" had already been achieved—now have to admit that it is still too early. If, however, even if it is only for the moment, conditions are such that capitalism and its juridical "superstructure," private property, cannot be dispensed with, can one say of an ideology that considers private property the foundation of society that it serves only to promote the selfish interests of the owners of capital against the interests of everyone else?

To be sure, if the antiliberal ideologies treat private property as indispensable, whether just for the present or forever, they believe, nevertheless, that it must be regulated and restricted by authoritarian decrees and similar acts of intervention on the part of the state. They recommend, not liberalism and capitalism, but interventionism. But economics has demonstrated that the system of interventionism is contrary to purpose and self-defeating. It cannot attain the ends that its advocates intend it to attain. Consequently, it is an error to suppose that besides socialism (communal property) and capitalism (private property) still a third system of organizing social cooperation is thinkable and workable, namely, interventionism. Attempts to put interventionism into effect must, of necessity, lead to conditions that run counter to the intentions of their authors, who are then faced with the alternative either of abstaining from all acts of intervention, and thereby leaving private property on its own, or of replacing private property by socialism.

This too is a thesis that liberal economists are not alone in maintaining. (Of course, the popular idea that economists are divided along party lines is altogether mistaken.) Marx too, in all his theoretical discussions, saw only the alternatives of socialism or capitalism and had nothing but derision and contempt for those reformers who, imprisoned in "petty-bourgeois thinking," reject socialism and, at the same time, still want to remodel capitalism. Economics has never even attempted to show that a system of private property regulated and restricted by government intervention would be practicable. When the "socialists of the chair" wanted to prove this at any cost, they began by denying the possibility of scientific knowledge in the economic field and ultimately ended by declaring that whatever the state does must surely be rational. Since science demonstrated the absurdity of the policy that they wished to recommend, they sought to invalidate logic and science.

The same is true of the proof of the possibility and practicability of socialism. The pre-Marxist writers had labored in vain to provide it. They could not do so, nor were they able in any way to attack the validity of the weighty objections to the practicability of their utopia that their critics based on the findings of science. Around the middle of the nineteenth century the socialist idea seemed already to have been effectively disposed of. Then Marx made his appearance. He did not, to be sure, adduce the proof—which, indeed, cannot be adduced—that socialism is realizable, but he simply declared—of course, without being able to demonstrate it—that the coming of socialism is inevitable. From this arbitrary assumption and from the axiom, which seemed to him self-evident, that everything occurring later in human history represents an advance over what came earlier, Marx drew the conclusion that socialism is therefore more perfect than capitalism and so there could naturally be no doubt as to its practicability. Consequently, it is altogether unscientific to concern oneself with the question of the possibility of a socialist society or even to study the problems of such a social order at all. Whoever wanted to try it was ostracized by the socialists and excommunicated by public opinion, which they controlled. Heedless of all these—to be sure, only external—difficulties, economics occupied itself with the theoretical construction of a socialist system and demonstrated irrefutably that every type of socialism is unworkable because economic calculation is impossible in a socialist community. The advocates of socialism have scarcely ventured to make any reply to this, and what they have advanced in rebuttal has been altogether trivial and devoid of significance.

What was proved by science theoretically was corroborated in practice by the failure of all socialist and interventionist experiments.

Hence, it is nothing but specious propaganda designed to rely for its effectiveness on the lack of judgment of the thoughtless to assert, as people do, that the defense of capitalism is purely an affair of the capitalists and the entrepreneurs, whose special interests, as opposed to those of other groups, are furthered by the capitalist system. The "have's" do not have any more reason to support the institution of private ownership of the means of production than do the "have-not's." If their immediate *special* interests come into question, they are scarcely liberal. The notion that, if only capitalism is preserved, the propertied classes could remain forever in possession of their wealth stems from a misunderstanding of the nature of the capitalist economy, in which property is continually being shifted from the less efficient to the more efficient businessman. In a capitalist society one can hold on to one's fortune only if one perpetually acquires it anew by investing it wisely. The rich, who are already in possession of wealth, have no special reason to desire the preservation of a system of unhampered competition open to all; particularly if they did not themselves earn their fortune, but inherited it, they have more to fear than to hope from competition. They do have a special interest in interventionism, which always has a tendency to preserve the existing division of wealth among those in possession of it. But they cannot hope for any special treatment from liberalism, a system in which no heed is paid to the time-honored claims of tradition advanced by the vested interests of established wealth.

The entrepreneur can prosper only if he provides what the consumers demand. When the world is afire with the lust for war, the liberal seeks to expound the advantages of peace; the entrepreneur, however, produces artillery and machine-guns. If public opinion today favors capital investment in Russia, the liberal may endeavor to explain that it is as intelligent to invest capital in a land whose government openly proclaims as the ultimate goal of its policy the expropriation of all capital as it would be to dump goods into the sea; but the entrepreneur does not hesitate to furnish supplies to Russia if only he is in a position to shift the risk to others, whether it be to the state or to some less clever capitalists, who allow themselves to be misled by public opinion, itself manipulated by Russian money. The liberal struggles against the trend towards commercial autarky; the German manufacturer, however, builds a factory in the eastern province, which excludes German goods, in order to serve this market while under the protection of the tariff. Clear-thinking entrepreneurs and capitalists may view the consequences of an antiliberal policy as ruinous for the whole of society; but in their capacity as entrepreneurs and capitalists they must seek, not to oppose it, but to adjust themselves to the given conditions.

There is no class that could champion liberalism for its own selfish interests to the detriment of the whole of society and the other strata of the population, simply because liberalism serves no special interest. Liberalism cannot count on the help that the antiliberal parties receive from the fact that everyone who seeks to win some privilege for himself at the expense of the rest of society attaches himself to them. When the liberal comes before the electorate as a candidate for public office and is asked by those whose votes he solicits what he or his party intends to do for them and their group, the only answer he can give is: Liberalism serves everyone, but it serves no special interest.

To be a liberal is to have realized that a special privilege conceded to a small group to the disadvantage of others cannot, in the long run, be preserved without a fight (civil war): but that, on the other hand, one cannot bestow privileges on the majority, since these then cancel one another out in their value for those whom they are supposed to specially favor, and the only net result is a reduction in the productivity of social labor.

# 5

# The Future of Liberalism

All earlier civilizations perished, or at least reached a state of stagnation, long before they had attained the level of material development that modern European civilization has succeeded in achieving. Nations were destroyed by wars with foreign enemies as well as by internecine strife. Anarchy forced a retrogression in the division of labor; cities, commerce, and industry declined; and, with the decay of their economic foundations, intellectual and moral refinements had to give way to ignorance and brutality. The Europeans of the modern age have succeeded in intensifying the social bonds among individuals and nations much more strongly than was ever the case before in history. This was an achievement of the ideology of liberalism, which, from the end of the seventeenth century, was elaborated with ever increasing clarity and precision and continually gained in influence over men's minds. Liberalism and capitalism created the foundations on which are based all the marvels characteristic of our modern way of life.

Now our civilization is beginning to scent a whiff of death in the air. Dilettantes loudly proclaim that all civilizations, including our own, must perish: this is an inexorable law. Europe's final hour has come, warn these prophets of doom, and they find credence. An autumnal mood is perceptibly beginning to set in everywhere.

But modern civilization will not perish unless it does so by its own act of self-destruction. No external enemy can destroy it the way the Spaniards once destroyed the civilization of the Aztecs, for no one on earth can match his strength against the standard-bearers of modern civilization. Only inner enemies can threaten it. It can come to an end only if the ideas of liberalism are supplanted by an antiliberal ideology hostile to social cooperation.

There has come to be a growing realization that material progress is possible only in a liberal, capitalist society. Even if this point is not expressly conceded by the antiliberal, it is fully acknowledged indirectly in the panegyrics extolling the idea of stability and a state of rest.

The material advances of recent generations, it is said, have, of course, been really very agreeable and beneficial. Now, however, it is time to call a halt. The frantic hustle and bustle of modern capitalism must make way for tranquil contemplation. One must acquire time for self-communion, and so another economic system must take the place of capitalism, one that is not always restlessly chasing after novelties and innovations. The romantic looks back nostalgically to the economic conditions of the Middle Ages—not to the Middle Ages as they actually were, but to an image of them constructed by his fancy without any counterpart in historical reality. Or he turns his gaze upon the Orient—again not, of course, the real Orient, but a dream-vision of his phantasy. How happy men were without modern technology and modern culture! How could we ever have renounced this paradise so light-mindedly?

Whoever preaches the return to simple forms of the economic organization of society ought to keep in mind that only our type of economic system offers the possibility of supporting in the style to which we have become accustomed today the number of people who now populate the earth. A return to the Middle Ages means the extermination of many hundreds of millions of people. The friends of stability and rest, it is true, say that one by no means has to go as far as that. It suffices to hold fast to what has already been achieved and to forgo further advances.

Those who extol the state of rest and stable equilibrium forget that there is in man, in so far as he is a thinking being, an inherent desire for the improvement of his material condition. This impulse cannot be eradicated; it is the motive power of all human action. If one prevents a man from working for the good of society while at the same time providing for the satisfaction of his own needs, then only one way remains open to him: to make himself richer and others poorer by the violent oppression and spoliation of his fellow men.

It is true that all this straining and struggling to increase their standard of living does not make men any happier. Nevertheless, it is in the nature of man continually to strive for an improvement in his material condition. If he is forbidden the satisfaction of this aspiration, he becomes dull and brutish. The masses will not listen to exhortations to be moderate and contented; it may be that the philosophers who preach such admonitions are laboring under a serious self-delusion. If one tells people that their fathers had it much worse, they answer that they do not know why they should not have it still better.

Now, whether it is good or bad, whether it receives the sanction of the moral censor or not, it is certain that men always strive for an improvement in their conditions and always will. This is man's inescapable destiny. The restlessness and inquietude of modern man is a stirring of the mind, the nerves, and the senses. One can as easily restore to him the innocence of childhood as lead him back to the passivity of past periods of human history.

But, after all, what is being offered in return for the renunciation of further material progress? Happiness and contentment, inner harmony and peace will not be created simply because people are no longer intent on further improvement in the satisfaction of their needs. Soured by resentment, the literati imagine that poverty and the absence of wants create especially favorable conditions for the development of man's spiritual capacities, but this is nonsense. In discussing these questions, one should avoid euphemisms and call things by their right names. Modern wealth expresses itself above all in the cult of the body: hygiene, cleanliness, sport. Today still the luxury of the well-to-do—no longer, perhaps, in the United States, but everywhere else—these will come within the reach of everyone in the not too distant future if economic development progresses as it has hitherto. Is it thought that man's inner life is in any way furthered by excluding the masses from the attainment of the level of physical culture that the well-to-do already enjoy? Is happiness to be found in the unkempt body?

To the panegyrists of the Middle Ages one can only answer that we know nothing about whether the medieval man felt happier than the modern man. But we may leave it to those who hold up the mode of life of the Orientals as a model for us to answer the question whether Asia is really the paradise that they describe it as.

The fulsome praise of the stationary economy as a social ideal is the last remaining argument that the enemies of liberalism have to fall back upon in order to justify their doctrines. Let us keep clearly in mind, however, that the starting-point of their critique was that liberalism and capitalism impede the development of productive forces, that they are responsible for the poverty of the masses. The opponents of liberalism have alleged that what they are aiming at is a social order that could create more wealth than the one they are attacking. And now, driven to the wall by the counterattack of economics and sociology, they must concede that only capitalism and liberalism, only private property and the unhampered activity of entrepreneurs, can guarantee the highest productivity of human labor.

It is often maintained that what divides present-day political parties is a basic opposition in their ultimate philosophical commitments that cannot be settled by rational argument. The discussion of these antagonisms must therefore necessarily prove fruitless. Each side will remain unshaken in its conviction because the latter is based on a comprehensive world view that cannot be altered by any considerations proposed by the reason. The ultimate ends toward which men strive are diverse. Hence, it is altogether out of the question that men aiming at these diverse ends could agree on a uniform procedure.

Nothing is more absurd than this belief. Aside from the few consistent ascetics, who seek to divest life of all its external trappings and who finally succeed in attaining to a state of renunciation of all desire and action and, indeed, of self-annihilation, all men of the white race, however diverse may be their views on supernatural matters, agree in preferring a social system in which labor is more productive to one in which it is less productive. Even those who believe that an ever progressing improvement in the satisfaction of human wants does no good and that it would be better if we produced fewer material goods— though it is doubtful whether the number of those who are sincerely of this opinion is very large—would not wish that the same amount of labor should result in fewer goods. At most, they would wish that there should be less labor and consequently less production, but not that the same amount of labor should produce less.

The political antagonisms of today are not controversies over ultimate questions of philosophy, but opposing answers to the question how a goal that all acknowledge as legitimate can be achieved most quickly and with the least sacrifice. This goal, at which all men aim, is the best possible satisfaction of human wants; it is prosperity and abundance. Of course, this is not all that men aspire to, but it is all that they can expect to attain by resort to external means and by way of social cooperation. The inner blessings—happiness, peace of mind, exaltation—must be sought by each man within himself alone.

Liberalism is no religion, no world view, no party of special interests. It is no religion because it demands neither faith nor devotion, because there is nothing mystical about it, and because it has no dogmas. It is no world view because it does not try to explain the cosmos and because it says nothing and does not seek to say anything about the meaning and purpose of human existence. It is no party of special interests because it does not provide or seek to provide any special advantage whatsoever to any individual or any group. It is something entirely different. It is an ideology, a doctrine of the mutual relationship among the members of society and, at the same time, the application of this doctrine to the conduct of men in actual society. It promises nothing that exceeds what can be accomplished in society and through society. It seeks to give men only one thing, the peaceful,

John Stuart Mill is an epigone of classical liberalism and, especially in his later years, under the influence of his wife, full of feeble compromises. He slips slowly into socialism and is the originator of the thoughtless confounding of liberal and socialist ideas that led to the decline of English liberalism and to the undermining of the living standards of the English people. Nevertheless—or perhaps precisely because of this—one must become acquainted with Mill's principal writings:

*Principles of Political Economy* (1848)
*On Liberty* (1859)
*Utilitarianism.* (1862)

Without a thorough study of Mill it is impossible to understand the events of the last two generations. For Mill is the great advocate of socialism. All the arguments that could be advanced in favor of socialism are elaborated by him with loving care. In comparison with Mill all other socialist writers—even Marx, Engels, and Lassalle—are scarcely of any importance.

One cannot understand liberalism without a knowledge of economics. For liberalism is applied economics; it is social and political policy based on a scientific foundation. Here, besides the writings already mentioned, one must familiarize oneself with the great master of classical economics:

David Ricardo, *Principles of Political Economy and Taxation* (1817).

The best introductions to the study of modern scientific economics are:

H. Oswalt, *Vorträge über wirtschaftliche Grundbegriffe* (many editions)
C. A. Verrijn Stuart, *Die Grundlagen der Volkswirtschaft* (1923).

The German masterpieces of modern economics are:

Carl Menger, *Grundsätze der Volkswirtschaftslehre* (first edition, 1871). An English translation of the first part of this work has been made available under the title, *Principles of Economics* (Glencoe, Ill., 1950).

Eugen von Böhm-Bawerk: *The Positive Theory of Capital* (New York, 1923). Also instructive is his *Karl Marx and the Close of His System* (New York, 1949).

The two most important contributions that Germany made to liberal literature suffered a misfortune no different from that which befell German liberalism itself. Wilhelm von Humboldt's *On the Sphere and Duties of Government* (London, 1854) lay completed in 1792. In the same year Schiller published an excerpt in the *Neuen Thalia,* and other excerpts appeared in the *Berliner Monatsschrift.* Since, however, Humboldt's publisher feared to issue the book, it was set aside, forgotten, and, only after the death of the author, discovered and published.

Hermann Heinrich Gossen's work, *Entwicklung der Gesetze des menschlichen Verkehrs und der daraus fliessenden Regeln für menschliches Handeln,* found a publisher, to be sure, but when it appeared in 1854 it attracted no readers. The work and its author remained forgotten until the Englishman Adamson came upon a copy.

Liberal thinking permeates German classical poetry, above all the works of Goethe and Schiller.

The history of political liberalism in Germany is brief and marked by rather meager success. Modern Germany—and this includes the defenders of the Weimar Constitution no less than their opponents—is a world apart from the spirit of liberalism. People in Germany no longer know what liberalism is, but they know how to revile it. Hatred of liberalism is the only point on which the Germans are united. Of the newer German writings on liberalism reference should be made to the works of Leopold von Wiese, *Der Liberalismus in Vergangenheit und Zukunft* (1917); *Staatssozialismus* (1916); and *Freie Wirtschaft* (1918).

Hardly a breath of the liberal spirit has ever reached the peoples of eastern Europe.

Although liberal thought is in decline even in western Europe and in the United States, one may yet call these nations liberal in comparison to the Germans.

Of the older liberal writers one should also read Frédéric Bastiat, *Oeuvres Complètes* (Paris, 1855). Bastiat was a brilliant stylist, so that the reading of his writings affords a quite genuine pleasure. In view of the tremendous advances that economic theory has made since his death, it is not astonishing that his teachings are obsolete today. Yet his critique of all protectionist and related tendencies is even today unsurpassed. The protectionists and interventionists have not been able to advance a single word in pertinent and objective rejoinder. They just continue to stammer: Bastiat is "superficial."

In reading the more recent political literature in English, one must not ignore the fact that in England today the word "liberalism" is frequently understood as denoting a moderate socialism. A concise presentation of liberalism is given by the Englishman, L. T. Hobhouse, *Liberalism* (1911), and by the American, Jacob H. Hollander, *Economic Liberalism* (1925). Even better introductions to the mind of the English liberals are:

Hartley Withers, *The Case for Capitalism* (1920).
Ernest J. P. Benn, *The Confessions of a Capitalist* (1925). *If I Were a Labor Leader* (1926). *The Letters of an Individualist* (1927). The last-named book includes a bibliography (pp. 74 *et seq.*) of the English literature on the basic problems of the economic system. *The Return to Laisser Faire* (London, 1928).

A critique of protectionist policy is presented by Francis W. Hirst in *Safeguarding and Protection* (1926).

Also instructive is the record of the public debate held in New York on January 23, 1931, between E. R. A. Seligmann and Scott Nearing on the topic: "That capitalism has more to offer to the workers of the United States than has socialism."

Introductions to sociological thought are provided by Jean

Izoulet, *La cité moderne* (first edition, 1890), and R. M. MacIver, *Community* (1924).

The history of economic ideas is presented by Charles Gide and Charles Rist, *Histoire des doctrines économiques* (many editions); Albert Schatz, *L'individualisme économique et social* (1907); and Paul Barth, *Die Geschichte der Philosophie als Soziologie* (many editions).

The role of political parties is treated by Walter Sulzbach in *Die Grundlagen der politischen Parteibildung* (1921).

Oskar Klein-Hattingen, *Geschichte des deutschen Liberalismus* (1911/1912, two volumes) provides an essay on the history of German liberalism, and Guido de Ruggiero does the same for liberalism in Europe in *The History of European Liberalism* (Oxford, 1927).

Finally, I cite my own works in so far as they stand in close connection with the problems of liberalism:

*Nation, Staat und Wirtschaft: Beiträge zur Politik und Geschichte der Zeit* (1919).

*Antimarxismus (Weltwirtschaftliches Archiv,* Vol. XXI, 1925).

*Kritik des Interventionismus* (1929).

*Socialism* (1936).

*Omnipotent Government* (1944).

*Human Action* (1949).

*The Anti-Capitalistic Mentality* (1956).

## 2. On the Term "Liberalism"

Those who are familiar with the writings on the subject of liberalism that have appeared in the last few years and with current linguistic usage will perhaps object that what has been called liberalism in the present volume does not coincide with what is understood by that term in contemporary political literature. I am far from disputing this. On the contrary! I have myself expressly pointed out that what is understood by the term "liberalism" today, especially in Germany, stands in direct opposition to what the history of ideas must designate as "liberalism" because it constituted the essential content of the liberal program of the eighteenth and nineteenth centuries. Almost all who call themselves "liberals" today decline to profess themselves in favor of private ownership of the means of production and advocate measures partly socialist and partly interventionist. They seek to justify this on the ground that the essence of liberalism does not consist in adherence to the institution of private property, but in other things, and that these other things demand a further development of liberalism, so that it must today no longer advocate private ownership of the means of production but instead either socialism or interventionism.

As to just what these "other things" might be, these pseudo liberals have yet to enlighten us. We hear much about humanity, magnanimity, real freedom, etc. These are certainly very fine and noble sentiments, and everyone will readily subscribe to them. And, in fact, every ideology does subscribe to them. Every ideology—aside from a few cynical schools of thought—believes that it is championing humanity, magnanimity, real freedom, etc. What distinguishes one social doctrine from another is not the ultimate goal of universal human happiness, which they all aim at, but the way by which they seek to attain this end. The characteristic feature of liberalism is that it proposes to reach it by way of private ownership of the means of production.

But terminological issues are, after all, of secondary importance. What counts is not the name, but the thing signified by it. However fanatical may be one's opposition to private property, one must still concede at least the possibility that someone may be in favor of it. And if one concedes this much, one will, of course, have to have some name to designate this school of thought. One must ask those who today call themselves liberals what name they would give to an ideology that advocates the preservation of private ownership of the means of production. They will perhaps answer that they wish to call this ideology "Manchesterism." The word "Manchesterism" was originally coined as a term of derision and abuse. Nevertheless, this would not stand in the way of its being employed to designate the liberal ideology if it were not for the fact that this expression has hitherto always been used to denote the economic rather than the general program of liberalism.

The school of thought that advocates private ownership of the means of production must in any case also be granted a claim to some name or other. But it is best to adhere to the traditional name. It would create only confusion if one followed the new usage that allows even protectionists, socialists, and warmongers to call themselves "liberal" when it suits them to do so.

The question could rather be raised whether, in the interest of facilitating the diffusion of liberal ideas, one ought not to give the ideology of liberalism a new name, so that the general prejudice fostered against it, especially in Germany, should not stand in its way. Such a suggestion would be well-intentioned, but completely antithetic to the spirit of liberalism. Just as liberalism must, from inner necessity, eschew every trick of propaganda and all the underhanded means of winning general acceptance favored by other movements, so it must also avoid abandoning its old name simply because it is unpopular. Precisely because the word "liberal" has a bad connotation in Germany, liberalism must stick to it. One may not make the way to liberal thinking easier for anyone, for what is of importance is not that men declare themselves liberals, but that they become liberals and think and act as liberals.

A second objection that can be raised against the terminology used in this book is that liberalism and democracy are not here conceived as opposites. Today in Germany "liberalism" is often taken to mean the doctrine whose political ideal is the constitutional monarchy, and "democracy" is understood as that which takes as its political ideal the parliamentary monarchy of the republic. This view is, even historically, altogether untenable. It was the parliamentary, not the constitutional, monarchy that liberalism strove for, and its defeat in this regard consisted precisely in the fact that in the German Empire and in Austria it was able to achieve only a constitutional monarchy. The triumph of antiliberalism lay in the fact that the German Reichstag was so weak that it might be accurately, if not politely, characterized as a "babblers' club," and the conservative party leader who said that a lieutenant and twelve men would suffice to dissolve the Reichstag was speaking the truth.

Liberalism is the more comprehensive concept. It denotes an ideology embracing all of social life. The ideology of democracy encompasses only that part of the realm of social relationships that refers to the constitution of the state. The reason why liberalism must necessarily demand democracy as its political corollary was demonstrated in the first part of this book. To show why all antiliberal movements, including socialism, must also be antidemocratic is the task of investigations that undertake to provide a thorough analysis of the character of these ideologies. In regard to socialism, I have attempted this in my book of that title.

It is easy for a German to go astray here, for he thinks always of the National Liberals and the Social Democrats. But the National Liberals were not, even from the outset—at least in matters of constitutional law—a liberal party. They were that wing of the old liberal party which professed to take its stand on "the facts as they really are"; that is, which accepted as unalterable the defeat that liberalism had sustained in the Prussian constitutional conflict from the opponents on the "Right" (Bismarck) and on the "Left" (the followers of Lassalle). The Social Democrats were democratic only so long as they were not the ruling party; that is, so long as they still felt themselves not strong enough to suppress their opponents by force. The moment they thought themselves the strongest, they declared themselves—as their writers had always asserted was advisable at this point—for dictatorship. Only when the armed bands of the Rightist parties had inflicted bloody defeats on them did they again become democratic "until further notice." Their party writers express this by saying: "In the councils of the social democratic parties, the wing which declared for democracy triumphed over the one which championed dictatorship."

Of course, the only party that may properly be described as democratic is one that under all circumstances—even when it is the strongest and in control—champions democratic institutions.

# Notes

NOTE TO THE INTRODUCTION

1. Leon Trotsky, *Literature and Revolution*, trans. by R. Strunsky (London, 1925), p. 256.

NOTES TO CHAPTER 2

1. Syndicalism as an end and as a social idea is not to be confused with syndicalism as a trade-union tactic (the "direct action" of the French syndicalists). Of course, the latter can serve as a means in the struggle for the realization of the syndicalist ideal, but it can also be made to serve other ends incompatible with that ideal. One can strive, for example— and this is precisely what some of the French syndicalists hope to do— to achieve socialism by resorting to syndicalist tactics.

2. Even if wages were artificially raised (by intervention on the part of the government or by coercion on the part of the trade unions), simultaneously throughout the whole world and in all branches of production, the result would simply be capital consumption and ultimately, as a further consequence of the latter, a still further reduction in wages. I have treated this question in detail in the writings listed in the appendix.

# Index

*Prepared by Vernelia A. Crawford*

*Note:* This index includes titles of chapters and divisions, each listed under the appropriate subject classification. With the exception of these specific page references, which are hyphenated, the numbers in each instance refer to the *first* page of a discussion. A page number followed by a figure in parentheses indicates the number of a footnote reference.

Ludwig von Mises was born on September 29, 1881. He grew up and was educated in Vienna and in 1900 entered the University of Vienna, where he received the degree of Doctor of Jurisprudence in 1906. At the University he studied with Friedrich von Wieser and Eugen von Böhm-Bawerk, the students of Carl Menger, who was the founder of the Austrian School of economics.

In 1913, shortly after the publication of his remarkable and erudite work *The Theory of Money and Credit,* Mises was named Professor Extraordinary at the University of Vienna. In 1926, he toured the United States under the sponsorship of the Laura Spelman Rockefeller Memorial. When he returned to Austria in 1926, he established the Austrian Institute for Business Cycle Research. In 1934, Mises accepted the offer of a professorship at the Graduate Institute of International Studies in Geneva.

In 1940, he immigrated to the United States and from 1940 to 1944, he was a guest of the National Bureau of Economic Research in New York. He did not return to teaching until 1945, when he was appointed Visiting Professor at the Graduate School of Business Administration, New York University.

By 1969, when he retired from teaching, he had established himself as one of the most prolific scholars of the twentieth century. A complete bibliography of his work would include twenty-two books and monographs (not counting translations and revised editions), plus more than 250 articles and reviews in journals, *Festschriften,* and other volumes. During his career he received the honorary degrees of Doctor of Laws (Grove City College, 1957), Doctor of Laws (New York University, 1963), and Doctor of Political Science (University of Freiburg, 1964). Shortly before his university retirement, Mises was named a Distinguished Fellow of the American Economic Association. He died on October 10, 1973.

The Studies in Economic Theory Series

*America's Great Depression,* by Murray N. Rothbard
ISBN: 0634-7 (cloth); 0647-9 (paper)

*The Economic Point of View,* by Israel M. Kirzner
ISBN: 0656-8 (cloth); 0657-6 (paper)

*The Economics of Ludwig von Mises: Toward a Critical Reappraisal,*
edited with an introduction by Laurence S. Moss
ISBN: 0650-9 (cloth); 0651-7 (paper)

*The Foundations of Modern Austrian Economics,* edited with an introduction
by Edwin G. Dolan
ISBN: 0653-3 (cloth); 0647-9 (paper)

*Capital, Interest, and Rent: Essays in the Theory of Distribution,* by
Frank A. Fetter, edited with an introduction by Murray N. Rothbard
ISBN: 0684-3 (cloth); 0685-1 (paper)

*Economics as a Coordination Problem: The Contributions of Friedrich A.
Hayek,* by Gerald P. O'Driscoll, Jr.
ISBN: 0662-2 (cloth); 0663-0 (paper)

*Capital, Expectations, and the Market Process: Essays on the Theory of
the Market Economy,* by Ludwig M. Lachmann, edited by Walter E. Grinder
ISBN: 0684-3 (cloth); 0685-1 (paper)

*The Ultimate Foundation of Economic Science,* by Ludwig von Mises
ISBN: 5101-6 (cloth); 5100-8 (paper)

*New Directions in Austrian Economics,* edited by Louis M. Spadaro
ISBN: 5104-0 (cloth); 5103-2 (paper)

If you are unable to obtain these books from your local bookseller, they may
be ordered direct from the publisher.

Sheed Andrews and McMeel, Inc.
6700 Squibb Road
Mission, Kansas 66202